THE SECRET WISDOM OF KUKULKAN

www.JoshuaPWarren.com

THE SECRET WISDOM OF KUKULKAN

Inter-dimensional Contact in a Holosentient Universe

by Joshua P. Warren

SHADOWBOX PUBLICATIONS
a division of Shadowbox Enterprises, LLC
www.ShadowboxENT.com

ISBN 978-0-578-03394-5

Shadowbox Enterprises, LLC
P. O. Box 16801
Asheville, North Carolina 28816
USA

www.ShadowboxENT.com

For Mobius, the Manifestor

Just remember that you're standing on a planet that's evolving
And revolving at nine hundred miles an hour,
That's orbiting at nineteen miles a second, so it's reckoned,
A sun that is the source of all our power.
The sun and you and me and all the stars that we can see
Are moving at a million miles a day
In an outer spiral arm, at forty thousand miles an hour,
Of the galaxy we call the "Milky Way."

Our galaxy itself contains a hundred billion stars.
It's a hundred thousand light years side to side.
It bulges in the middle, sixteen thousand light years thick,
But out by us, it's just three thousand light years wide.
We're thirty thousand light years from galactic central point.
We go 'round every two hundred million years,
And our galaxy is only one of millions of billions
In this amazing and expanding universe.

The universe itself keeps on expanding and expanding
In all of the directions it can whiz,
As fast as it can go, the speed of light, you know,
Twelve million miles a minute, and that's the fastest speed there is.
So remember, when you're feeling very small and insecure,
How amazingly unlikely is your birth,
And pray that there's intelligent life somewhere up in space,
'Cause there's bugger all down here on Earth.

~Monty Python
The Galaxy Song

What is knowing?

All that we see or seem
Is but a dream within a dream.

~Edgar Allen Poe

TABLE OF CONTENTS

CHAPTER ONE
What Are You?

IF I took a mighty hand and squashed every bit of water and empty space from your body, you would be the size of a pea I could roll between my fingers. Most of you is nothing. That is why so much will pass through your empty spaces. Radio waves, x-rays, magnetic fields, and so on, slip right through you. A loose cluster of matter has adhered to us, but we are so ego-centric that we usually think of ourselves as a solid and ultimate mass. As time advances, and knowledge grows, we understand more and more that we are less and less.

So what are you? You are one, infinitely tiny pinpoint of awareness, surrounded by an ever-changing energy field. And yet that quantum speck, *that is you*, can funnel and channel vast information from the sprawling cosmos, and from unimaginable dimensions. The seat of your being, consciousness, and awareness, is an infinitesimally small wormhole, and what you know is the information that flows through it—in and out—connecting the energy fields flowing and standing around it. You are a faucet and drain, pouring forth data and receiving it. That is the permanent you that has always been and will always be. Anything else extending from you is temporary, fluctuating, and bound to perpetual cycles of growth and decay in many, various forms.

This tube of information exchange—the dynamic seat of your consciousness—we will call the Wormhole Brian, or WHB. Though all are similar, no two are exactly alike. Some are larger or smaller than others, able to transfer more or less. The way in which the information is ultimately processed includes the filters of your physical brain, or lack thereof (as in single-celled organisms). Though the Wormhole Brains of you, an eagle, a bear, and a shark are equally impressive, the physical brain determines how that initial flow of cosmic information should be used—what is relevant to that particular creature's survival at that particular time, in that particular place. For example, at the Wormhole Brain level, you are not necessarily more intelligent than a dog, but the dog's physical brain extracts the information most suitable for the dog's survival needs, just as yours extracts the information suitable for a human. And yes, when one creature's form dies, it may eventually congeal, or reincarnate, into another creature's form. But there is really no such thing as death, just decay and transformation.

Your life in this realm, as a mature, self-contained soul, begins the moment you are separated from your mother, and no longer dependent on her alone for immediate survival. Your life, in this realm, as a mature, self-contained soul, ends the moment your consciousness fully detaches from your energy mold. These are the points when you transition through incarnations, and since all things in the universe are connected, the pattern of the stars and planets can signify things about your cycle. Astrology is based on time-worn observation of cycles and outcomes, hence its ability to define characteristics of your incarnations.

You don't necessarily remember your past selves. There's no point in it, as there have been more incarnations of you than sand grains upon the beaches. You may catch a glimpse of your recent incarnations once in a while, but it's not worth focusing on, anymore than focusing on an old car, now that you have a better one. And if it's not better, it's your job to make it better; to create what you WANT.

In the periods of time between your incarnations, the energy field around your Wormhole Brain is shaped like a sphere. You literally appear as a ball of light. The sphere is the most perfect, balanced, and efficient form. Photographers capture "orbs" created by specks of dust, moisture, reflections, etc., but *true orbs*—the ones that move slowly on video, passing through walls, brightening and dimming, bouncing and interacting—are discarnate beings. They are Wormhole Brains, surrounded by a basic energy field, and their interests are as varied as those of species within the animal kingdom. Are they good? Are they bad? It all depends on who is asking the question. You may as well ask the same question of all the people living on your street. Different people would give a different answer. But there is one universal truth: All beings first consider self-interest. If you contribute to the self-interest of a being, you are good to that being, if you do not, you are bad. Of course, there is a wide spectrum of shades in-between, and that is why relationships are so intricate and complex. "Good" and "bad" are subjective and culturally influenced terms. You must decide what is good or evil based on what harms others, while respecting others' rights to harm themselves to some degree.

Like all things, a Wormhole Brain can become infected, especially the joint where it extends into the energy field that becomes your physical brain and body. Sometimes this infection is due to a parasite—a discarnate Wormhole Brain that forces itself into the base of your energy field. This is traditionally called *possession*. That is generally too powerful a word, since the individual is not entirely possessed, but strongly influenced. This can happen most easily when the person's Wormhole Brain becomes weak due to lack of mental exercise, or because it opens too widely due to *irresponsible* use of mind-altering substances like drugs or alcohol.

When someone becomes possessed, removing the invasive Wormhole Brain can be a challenge. The key is to find what the invader fears or finds unpleasant. Subjecting it to that will eventually work. For example, if the parasite believes in a God that will damn one to hell, making threats in the name of God can work. If the parasite thrives on the energy of alcohol, avoid alcohol, and it will eventually leave to locate another source. That is why helping someone regain control begins with understanding the conditions that led up to the possession, and then how the parasite has been fed since then. To maintain control of yourself, spend considerable time each day exercising your intellect by reading about philosophy, science, and history, or working on puzzles and creative compositions of positive music or art. Those tasks provide well-rounded challenges to keep you mentally alert and fit.

Inevitably, over time, your present human body will decay and die. Do not be depressed as you watch your body weaken. Keep your mind strong. And you can help minimize the impact of watching your form decay by visiting "sacred sites." These are places that energize and excite you. Most of them have places that allow your brain to relax and slip into peaceful states. Any muscle clenched too long will tire. Your energy should be replenished once in a while. Sacred sites are places where the earth gives forth high-frequency fields, massaging and rejuvenating yours. They can be huge, exotic and famous, or a nook you've been lucky enough to find near your house. Most of them are near water. Enormous ruins, like the pyramids, were usually built near water. We'll explore that more later. Personally, I go into water to re-energize. My favorite place is a special bay in Puerto Rico.

Because we are an energy field, fed by a tiny wormhole, we are able to influence, and be influenced by, other energy fields. Other people, beings, objects, and places in nature impact us, and we impact them. This is called the Mind-Body-Environment connection, or MBE.

Paranormal investigation is so difficult because researchers are usually implementing extremely sensitive devices, hoping they can measure some subtle field. But the more subtle the field, the more it is drowned by the researcher's equipment and very presence. Much paranormal activity only transpires in the physical presence of an observer. If the investigator leaves the site, the activity may not occur. Remote cameras play an unclear role in this process since they are actually extensions of the researcher's physical presence.

I'm talking about a subject that can be viewed from two extremes. Firstly, when you walk into a room, you carry with you a storm of electromagnetic energy. Tiny lightning bolts of electrostatic charge shoot around you every moment, making changes in the room that we may not notice during the daily distraction of a routine walk, but nonetheless distort the energy environment significantly.

Every object in the world, including your body, maintains a property called *isotropic capacitance*. You see, we generally think of a world filled with conductors (things that allow electricity to pass) and non-conductors or insulators (things that do not allow electricity to pass). But the fact is that everything is actually dielectric, meaning, in my terminology, it is capable of conducting some electrical energy within certain parameters. We simply call the ones that conduct the best "conductors" and those that conduct the worst "insulators."

Since every bit of physical mass is transferring energy all the time, when you walk into a room, there are overlapping fields of energy between you and every object in the room. It's the same when you step outside; your body is somehow touching every tree, each cloud, each stone and blade of grass. You are connected to the world around you. The strength of that connection is powerful and direct. But it is so complex that we can't yet fathom all the webs, nor account for all the variables, changing every second, by the billions, as you simply move, think, and exist in this world. Sure, properties like humidity affect the degree of interaction, but a lightning bolt forms in rain because the power of the bolt is greater than the amount of moisture that can diffuse it. Some people, and energies, are stronger than others.

But furthermore, to fully appreciate the Mind-Body-Environment connection, you must consider the wisdom of quantum physics. The Heisenberg Uncertainty Principle has proven that by merely observing something, you influence or change what is being observed. You may not understand the full implications of that yet, but you will. Think about what it means. By existing, by observing, you create change in the world. Like it or not, for better or for worse, *you are a creator*. What do you create each day?

CHAPTER TWO

Where Are You?

YOU ARE bathing in a timeless ocean of electromagnetic energy, congealed into patterns and forms in a constant state of flux. Some things move quickly, others move slowly. A plant appears to stand still, but if you videotape it all day, then play back the recording at high speed, you will see the plant moves quite a bit. Even the rocks are vibrating and changing at their smallest levels. An insect moves quickly, but doesn't live long. A turtle moves slowly, but lives a long time. The brain of a roach or housefly processes information so quickly that we look like lumbering giants moving in slow motion to them. That's why it's so hard to swat or stomp them.

Very simply, life is the result of motion. All this talk about energy means: energy is the ability to do work. Work is the result of change. Change occurs from motion. Therefore, motion is the key to it all. That is why you will always be in motion. There is no ultimate destination when all finally stops. That would be true death. We do not live in a dead universe. There is no state of perfection—no true divinity—no final homecoming in paradise—because that would be an inactive, unmotivated state of utter, eternal deadness.

The world in which we live is composed of many layers, similar to an onion, just like yourself. Let's look at the three basic layers. The first is the Resistance Layer.

<u>Resistance Layer:</u> This is the slowest, crudest layer of general

human experience. It is the medium for strict Newtonian mechanics. When I push on the wall, my hand does not pass through because of this layer. Objects resist each other the same way like poles of a magnet push apart, or two like electrostatic charges repel each other. This is the part that is dense, where there is enough matter clustered around the fields so that the bits of matter block each other. This is the layer that allows you to predict the way balls will strike and affect each other on a pool table. Explanations for most phenomena visible to people are contained at this level.

<u>Boundary Layer:</u> If I drag my shoes across the carpet on a dry day, then touch your shoulder to deliver an electrostatic shock, you're seeing the Boundary Layer at work. This is the fuzzy edge of exchanging particles that surround all objects. If you zoom into a photograph, the magnified image eventually reveals a hazy boundary of pixels on lines that appear solid at a distance. This effect exists in physical reality, as well. You are constantly trading bits of energy and information with everything around you, as are all objects. This is the layer at which all things that may appear separate actually merge into one undulating mass of animation when examined closely.

<u>Dimensional Layer:</u> This is the layer of reality that contains phenomena we experience, but cannot yet measure beyond the raw human perception. For example, the ability to move your arm by simply desiring the action is dimensional input. Your imagination, memories, and emotions exist on the dimensional realm. We can measure side-effects of this layer on the lower realms (such as electrical impulses it creates), but we cannot document the dimensional layers themselves. These are extremely high, or extremely low, frequencies, and contain a realm that may harbor infinite levels. Current physicists believe there are at least eight dimensions beyond the physical three we generally think about

day-to-day. You cannot truly understand higher dimensions, but you can experience them.

In his 1884 book *Flatland*, English scholar Edwin Abbott described the challenges of a 2-D being trying to comprehend a 3-D one. The 3-D figure's entrance into Flatland manifests in ways that are completely paranormal to the 2-D being. And this is beautifully described in an online video by Carl Sagan (do a net search on "Carl Sagan" and "Flatland").

Physicality is completely relative. Two things are only physical to each other if they both occupy a similar frequency range. Radio waves pass through you because your frequency is so different. But if your frequency were closer to that of a radio wave, you would feel the waves like a physical force, and they would not pass through you. You would encounter them like a wall in a house. The same goes for all frequencies we know of (alpha, beta, gamma, x-rays, microwaves, etc). There are surely billions of frequencies we do not know about in the world of human science.

Science is designed to solve the simplest mysteries first, and provide a model of reality that is the most useful for survival. Science has done a fine job in this regard. But never think of "science" as a "conclusion." It is a method of exploration. The scientific process is not meant to provide the truth, but to provide a model of reality consistent with *most* of the observations. The word "most" is key here. If a scientist repeats an experiment and gets the same result 99% of the time, and receives a totally different result 1% of the time, it's easier for the scientist to throw out that 1% as a mistake or fluke instead of re-doing the 99%. This is a common aspect of human nature, and scientists are very human, especially if working to pay bills. Never forget that the world around you is vast and complex beyond comprehension. Do not make the common mistake of believing the purpose of science is to determine what is and what is not possible. The purpose of science is to obtain specific and limited answers to specific and limited questions under specific and limited conditions.

Within this incomprehensible scope of oscillating energy, far beyond the perception of current scientific capability, you will find surprising and wondrous things. We break everything, including your cells, down into molecules. We break molecules down into atoms. And within atoms there are even smaller particles that pop in and out of our reality. They literally appear, disappear, then appear again. Modern scientists have no idea where they go. Here is the answer:

For many years, the concept of a black hole was a part of science fiction. Astoundingly, in the early 2000s, it was confirmed that a black hole is at the center of our galaxy, and probably *all* other galaxies. A tiny black hole also exists within each individual atom, hence the ability for particles to pop in and out. Your world, however large or small the scale of observation, consists of information constantly transferring between the Resistance Layer and Dimensional Layer. Every time this happens, there is a subtle effect in the Boundary Layer. Energy is always traveling back and forth. All consist of miniature Wormhole Brains, and the face of the Wormhole Brain is the black hole.

So, on grand and tiny scales, we have a vast slate of black holes, attached to wormholes, exchanging information between our Resistance Layer and Dimensional Layer, with measurable effects in the Boundary Layer. So precisely how can we be certain of this?

I know a scientist who conducted an interesting experiment regarding capacitors. A capacitor is a simple device that stores tiny electrical charges up to a critical point when there is eventually one large discharge. Imagine this: The most basic capacitor (also called a condenser) is a piece of plastic that separates two pieces of aluminum foil. As a boy, I used to take plastic whip cream containers and put a piece of foil on the outside and inside, making sure the pieces of foil did not touch each other. I would then gradually apply electrical charges to one of the pieces of foil (using a simple device called an electrophorus—made from a metal jar lid and wax candle). After a while, I could touch both pieces of foil at the same time to receive a shock.

The scientist I knew took a piece of plastic, with two pieces of metal foil on either side, and applied a charge to the foil. He then removed the foil from the plastic and measured the foil. The metal had no charge. Next, he stuck them back on the plastic, then touched both of them. They produced an electric discharge. He had proven that the charge is not stored in the conductors (metals) but the insulator (the plastic). He then went on to test this setup in a vacuum, simply placing the two pieces of metal close together, without the plastic in-between. He found the capacitor still worked in the vacuum. If we know the pieces of foil do not hold the charge, and in a vacuum there is not one single measurable bit of matter between them, where is the charge being stored? The charge is being stored in the medium of space-time itself, often called Zero Point Energy (or ZPE).

Bearing this in mind, the basic model of electricity presented in grammar school books is inherently flawed. If electrical potential is stored in non-conductors, with molecules spread far apart, like plastic, and simply transferred by conductors, with molecules close together, like metal, then you must re-envision the world around you. See your surroundings like a negative image. Each metal object is a vacant bubble. Each plastic object is buzzing with energy. All objects in-between possess various degrees of energy. The less dense, the more energy. The more dense, the less energy. The most energy is in the empty vacuum of space-time—the canvas of reality.

As I write this, the medium of space-time, what some call the *ether*, is so misunderstood that it can hardly be defined. However, we walk and move within this background ocean of infinite energy that can be tapped. It both stores and expels incredible power. Places on earth at which it naturally expels energy are sites where "paranormal" phenomena most easily occur.

There may be ghosts, aliens, and inter-dimensionals everywhere. However, in order for them to be easily observed by us, they must be energized. The places on our planet where they are observed are hot spots. And if we study those hot spots properly, we can learn how that energy bursts forth naturally, and how we can tap into it, so it bursts forth at our command. That is why the military is interested in paranormal hot spots. Military does not have to justify interests for philosophical purposes; they are mainly interested in the practical protection of people by using what works. And tapping into energy from the vacuum, without bringing a heavy, clumsy power source along, is a dream come true.

There seem to be bursts of energy that surge from our planet once in a while. These are most likely what create natural crop circles. Every moment, hundreds of lightning bolts are striking the planet somewhere, playing it like a huge drum. If, from time to time, a powerful harmonic frequency culminates and exits, it may leave in its wake a fantastic pattern, like so many created in the lab by sprinkling sand over a speaker and playing various notes and tones. Some of the bursts would be low enough to fill the microwave range, explaining why the joints of some crop circles hay are blown out, as if the water locked inside has been quickly boiled and expanded, rupturing the hay structure and loosening molecules so the hay temporarily "melts" over in a semi-liquid state.

The earth is covered in a network of energy flows. Many call them ley lines. Your own body is a representation of the earth and cosmos. Just as electrical energy condenses and flows among the points of least resistance on your body, so does it flow around our planet. A massive grid of energy circuits exist. At certain places, they condense and swirl, connecting our planet to the cosmos. Those points where the grids connect and surge into the galaxy are called vortexes. We do not currently have the technology to measure these points, but they are felt by sensitive humans. I have visited the ley lines and vortexes of Sedona, Arizona and Western North Carolina in the United States. Those are spots where humans are drawn to re-energize from the planet's circuitry. Place your finger at the site of Egypt on a globe and spin it around. You will find your finger crosses the locations of earth's most significant pyramids and important ancient structures, reaching to the heavens. Ancient people were aware of these energy lines, though they were supposedly separate and independent cultures. On the other hand, some earth sites, like Brown Mountain, North Carolina, are so full of powerful energy that plasma lights, similar to ball lightning, appear and float around; these places emit enough energy to trigger all kinds of strange phenomena on levels considered psychological and physical.

Though the energy from the vacuum, accessible via ley lines, is still elusive, some researchers have found media by which humans can directly manipulate global forces. One of the most outstanding was Wilhelm Reich, pioneer of *orgone* energy. Reich, a man with an impressive background, realized that, aside from empty space, humans are mainly water. And, of course, the surface layer of our planet (including the atmosphere and weather) is ruled by water. Molecules of water interact with each other in strange ways. Drops of water running down a car windshield attract to each other, a phenomenon called *cohesion*. And flowing water produces an enormous amount of electrical energy. The English physicist, Lord Kelvin, was enthralled by this, and produced a demonstration, now called Kelvin's Thunderstorm, in which he showed that falling drops of water could amass impressive electrical shocks.

Reich considered the relationship between humans, atmospheric water, and the basis of all organic materials, this energy field called *orgone*. The term *orgone* was based on the human orgasm—foundation of human life. The simplest example of this energy was the ability for human consciousness to control the weather via "cloudbusting;" making clouds break up with a concentrated gaze. Have you ever tried this? If not, go outside, target a cloud, and stare at it intensely, imagining it breaking into pieces. It's not that hard to achieve, especially if you focus on a light, thin, fluffy cloud, as opposed to a tall, thick, dark one. Reich wanted to take this phenomenon to the next level.

We humans are tiny balloons of water on the face of an enormous water planet, with aquatic vapor flowing above. Reich realized that buildups of water would eventually fall to earth in the form of precipitation. He developed simple devices to manipulate that balance. For example, a series of metal pipes, attached to a river or stream and pointed at the sky (called *cloudbusters*), could gradually draw the orgone from the atmosphere and into the earth, preventing rain. On the other hand, orgone deficits could be created, eventually creating rain from orgone that filled the void. All of this was facilitated by the human consciousness, since we are living bodies of moisture. His research delved deeply into the mysteries of these mind-body-environment relationships through water. His orgone was similar to the fundamental bio-energy ancient cultures have called chi, ki, or prana. However, since his work was done systematically, and included defined information on how this could assist in human health, he died in prison, branded a quack and con man by those in the federal drug trade who clung to ad-hoc cures for capitalistic purposes. Many impressive minds have met this depressing outcome. Read about Royal Rife, whose machines treated most ailments known to man by isolating them and blasting them with specific electromagnetic frequencies, tuned to reshape them for the benefit of the patient. Like Reich, many still practice his work today.

You can also understand why cloudbuster technology has been suppressed. If you want a sunny day today, and your neighbor wants a sunny day next week, each of you battling with your cloudbusters would throw the entire system into disarray. After all, we do live in a bubble, and the forces must balance one way or another. When you try to cloudbust with your eyes, you may be amazed by how easily you can achieve results by shifting your conscious intent into the cloud. You are a bag of water with thoughts. Those thoughts can be transferred into other bodies of water. It's even easier when you have a group of people all focusing on the same goal. Some are so aware of water power that they only drink "charged water," infused with positive intent by psychics and shaman. Dr. Masaru Emoto experiments with how thoughts can shape water crystals into healthy forms, and even my company has produced the popular "Psychotronic Water" that employs this philosophy.

The idea of weather manipulation is controversial altogether, since every person on the planet is affected by one large, universal system. The Butterfly Effect reaches beyond what we can see. There are too many variables involved for us to keep up with, and that's why the concept of predicting weather, with all its complications, parallels the difficulty we have in predicting paranormal phenomena. Look at all the money and resources invested in weather prediction, yet we are still far from any model of success. The U.S. HAARP program in Alaska uses acres of tall antennas to broadcast extremely high wattage onto tiny portions of the earth's ionosphere. There is a natural balance of energy between the ionosphere and the planet, and focusing too much energy on the ionosphere forces a short circuit in the flow of energy between the two. Depending on the intensity of the projection, electromagnetic waves can be created that alter communications signals, and the moods and thoughts of humans in the middle of the energy transfer. This technology could cause enormous discharges, like a huge, city-sized lightning bolt vaporizing a population instantly. When used on a lesser scale, it can also change the temperature of weather systems, allowing for greater control of global temperatures. It's easy to see why such technology can never be fully exposed when it's being controlled by one government, and that particular government's needs may not always coincide with the needs of other countries.

A large part of Wilhelm Reich's work closely paralleled the electrical theory of capacitors. In the same way that layers of conductors and non-conductors would store energy, he explored layers of organic and inorganic materials. Layers of leaves and glass, or wool and steel, would naturally store and propel streams of the orgone energy. This could facilitate many aspects of human health and enlightenment, but to this day, the implications are buried beneath its side-effects measured through electricity, magnetism and temperature differential. Orgone energy may also play a role in basic *dowsing*, the usage of tools to help humans interact with the world around us.

CHAPTER THREE
Tools to Access Truth

ALBERT EINSTEIN said "The most important decision we make is whether we believe we live in a friendly or hostile universe." From that, perhaps we can extrapolate an even more substantive point: You must decide whether or not you are a mere, helpless doll at the whims of some powerful, impersonal force, or you are an active, engaging participant in your destiny, able to shape it to your liking. The dilemma of free will versus determinism has been debated by philosophers for centuries. But in practicality, on a personal level, the problem is solved for you if there are numerous predetermined outcomes for you, yet you are able to choose which one to experience most vividly.

If you believe you are solely a rag doll, batted around by impervious powers, then you may as well lie down and die today. However, we know empirically that you can pick yourself up and choose to develop. Therefore, if you choose to engage the universe around you, it's natural to seek assistance. The power structure of society places psychological boundaries on us from birth, limiting what we think we can achieve. Every time a baby pops forth into the world, everyone assumes it will most likely grow up to be a conditioned dumbass. After all, most of us are merely average—that's why it's *the average*! Therefore, most people treat you like a dumbass unless and until you prove otherwise. The easiest way to begin our process of overcoming those societal boundaries is with the assistance of tools—temporary crutches—that can gradually prove the possible to you, allowing you to transcend the borders so distinctly imposed.

There is a true gut instinct, deep within you, molded by millions of years, that responds to all stimuli around you. In the general sense, it functions as a binary code: relaxing and tensing. Everything you encounter, be it physical or mental, produces some gradient of contraction or relaxation. On a deep level, you produce a vibration around you composed of an organic morse code, your organs clenching and releasing, sometimes many times per second. Unfortunately, we cannot always be aware of these signals since we are taught, from birth, to function within the theater of culture. You are supposed to look, speak and behave in a certain way. Depending on the culture, some of these requirements are beneficial for the collective civilization and some are not. Regardless, a good deal of your attention is focused upon those standards instead of acknowledging how you feel within. Simple tools that help express how you feel within are called dowsing instruments.

Your body is an antenna for all the activity around it. A dowsing instrument is a simple device that takes a tiny reaction within your body and magnifies it into a more visible and dramatic expression. The simplest type of dowsing tool is a rod or pendulum. There are various methods of dowsing, but most rods are L-shaped wires, and one held in each hand swings to and fro in response to a question. Pendulums can be as simple as a fishing sinker tied to a bit of wire, hanging from between the fingers. Detailed info on these techniques, and developing telekinetic ability with a homemade energy wheel, are in my book *How to Hunt Ghosts*, so I won't get into the specifics of how to dowse here. I bring this all up for a greater point.

Regardless of how one chooses to dowse, the dowsing process is extremely personal, customized by the dowser. Successful dowsing begins with the dowser first deciding what is to be sought and gained from the dowsing, and then telling the dowsing tool how to respond (often called *programming*). So, for example, let's say an old timer want to find water with a forked stick. He must decide, or "tell" the stick what to do when water is encountered. Then he relaxes and strolls along until the stick responds. Actually, the stick itself is not necessarily responding, but his body is responding since he inherently, psychically knows where the water is, but cannot consciously access the information. The stick allows him to tap into his subconscious ability.

If you are dowsing with a pendulum to find the location of your lost car keys, you would tell the pendulum to swing clockwise for "yes" and counter-clockwise for "no." Then you would proceed to ask the pendulum, "are they in my garage? Are they in my bedroom?" until you get an affirmative response. You would then continue to break it down to the right area. Another person might apply the exact same technique, but tell the pendulum to swing counter-clockwise for "yes" and clockwise for "no." As you can see, in the process of dowsing, what is important is the programming of the instrument, deciding how psychic knowledge from the Wormhole Brain should be expressed by a visible tool. This is the basis for how tools work. In this sense, tools are ultimately devices that allow us to more easily document our interactions with the environment.

Upon accepting that dowsing is not about some strange physical interaction between a tool and environment (such as a forked stick and an underground stream) but the response of the body to information streaming from the Wormhole Brain, you can reduce the phenomenon to your individual ability. Science is based on things that most humans have in common. As we explore deeper, and things are more individualized and unique, science does not apply. That is why those consumed solely with science only understand the densest crust of human experience. Here, we take a fascinating turn:

Every item that is capable of receiving information is also capable of projecting it. For example, if you spin a magnet next to a coil of wire, the wire produces electricity (a generator). But if you apply electricity to the coil of wire, the magnet spins (a motor). A speaker can be reversed to create a microphone, and a microphone reversed to create a speaker. A large radio antenna can either stand passively to receive signals from electricity in the air, or it can broadcast electricity into the air so that other antennas will receive it. One of the best examples of how broadcasting works is the model of a swimming pool with a beach ball floating at both ends. When a person taps the ball at one end, ripples cross the water and the ball on the other end eventually bounces the same way. This can be done on either end, back and forth, demonstrating that either ball can be a sender or receiver. As with this example, you will find that all life's greatest mysteries are somehow exemplified by the small, and the small culminate in the large. The motion of atoms mimics the motion of star systems.

Since your Wormhole Brain can receive information useful for techniques like dowsing, it is also capable of powerfully broadcasting data into the universe. Just as change and variation is gathered and condensed, so is it projected and expanded. The idea that your immensely strong Wormhole Brain can be properly focused to send your desires into the ether is primarily where dowsing tools transform into radionic tools.

Radionic tools are divided into various subjects, like psionics or psychotronics. I suggest you dig into the specifics on your own. For that, I recommend some of the books by Charles Cosimano, such as *Psychic Power* and *Psionic Power*. But in a nutshell, think about how your life, thoughts, and brainwaves are shaped by mere symbols. One of the best examples is cash. If you're stranded in the desert with a pile of money, it's virtually useless. Yet if you're in a city where a vendor agrees the currency has some value, you can trade it for goods. Another example: let's say someone called you a dirty name and you wanted to punch that person. Now imagine the same scenario, except the person is wearing a badge. You would most likely be less apt to punch the badge-wearer, since that symbol represents a list of psychological implications that may, or may not be, accurate. These very words I write are mere symbols, and yet you are changing physically as you read them. Imagine how your body would respond if I merely told you a special loved one in your life had just died. Radionics is the study and implementation of symbolic tools that stimulate your mind to cause change in the universe. A part of radionics is sacred geometry, dealing with the fact that ancient cultures around the world used similar structures, like pyramids, to influence the mind. To this day, in the United States, we still have a pyramid on the dollar bill! However, there has never been an ancient pyramid found in the United States. Some symbols are so ubiquitous throughout history that they have defined mathematical staples. One mathematical ratio that constantly crops up in ancient architecture, art, and in fact, natural designs, is 1: 1.618. This is called the Golden Ratio or the Golden Mean. There is something about that ratio that triggers a flow of information from the human mind.

Radionic devices use time-proven symbols to help you send your wishes into the universe. This can be done through the usage of cool-looking machines covered in knobs and coils, or by simple drawings of the machines—let me repeat that: *drawings of the machines*. Imagine if you could heat up a potato by drawing a microwave and putting the potato on top of it. That doesn't work on the Boundary Layer of reality. But radionics taps into the Dimensional Layer. Basic radionic machines have plates where you put a sample to represent what you want to change, then some mechanism by which you change it. For example, one radionic box I own has a small metal plate where I could place one of your hairs. That hair represents you. Next I think about what I want to happen to you while I turn a bunch of dials, one by one, as I swing a pendulum over another plate, stopping each dial where the pendulum indicates the dial should stay. Once everything is in place, I leave the entire machine as is, and eventually my wishes will come true. Some call this a wishing machine. But don't forget, the whole machine can work if I simply draw it on a piece of paper. It doesn't have to be physically 3-D since it's not operating on the physical 3-D level.

I use the subject of radionics to transition to the subject of magick and thoughtforms. When it comes to tools, I have stressed that each kind is ultimately connected to the same source—the Wormhole Brain. Frankly, any tool that a human can create, including the most complex computer, is still connected to the Wormhole Brain, since a brain created it, operates it, and interprets its feedback. Therefore, if you want to get right down the purest form of tooling around—both sensing the environment and sending information into the universe to change it—it always boils right back down to your Wormhole Brain. Magicians have always known this, and that's why those folks eventually skip radionic machines and magic wands. They go right for pure visualization. Becoming a magician is about gradually training yourself to de-construct the limitations of culture and reconnect with your true inner power. It should be done in baby steps, so going through dowsing and radionics first is a wise way of transitioning from the Resistance Layer to the Dimensional Layer.

I don't think I need to say this, but alas, when I write of magicians, I'm not talking about illusionists who entertain. I'm speaking of people who perfect the art of affecting change in the universe, according to their will, at a faster rate than it would normally occur. Aleister Crowley popularized the spelling "magick" instead of "magic" to clarify that distinction. So how exactly does magick work?

If there is only one lesson you should take from this book, it is this: thoughts are real, tangible things that affect all levels of reality. Because we are distracted by the Resistance Layer, we too often consider thoughts to be an energy on the Dimensional Layer alone. That could not be farther from the truth. Thoughts impact the Resistance Layer just as much as the Dimensional or Boundary Layers. However, thoughts do not necessarily create instant change—they take time to resonate throughout the environment. This is why it's exceptionally rare for someone to be able to sit down and move a ping pong ball instantly at will. On the other hand, thoughts can move your body incredibly quickly, given your body's proximity to the thought. Each time you decide to move your arm, and your arm then moves, you are witnessing a form of telekinesis. Newtonian physics tells us that for every action there is an opposite but equal reaction. But this cannot explain how you move your body with a simple thought alone, unless thoughts actually do possess physical power. Indeed, they do.

Each thought of yours extends into the ocean of thoughts around it. A weak thought will quickly drop off and become diluted. A strong, concentrated thought can be just as condensed and effective as a bullet, though. Taking time to fashion a thought into a self-contained, penetrating vehicle, to be fired into the ether, is an extremely significant task. These capsules of intention are what we can call thoughtforms. A master magician knows how to quickly and efficiently create thoughtforms, then fire them into the ether, producing change with great effectiveness.

Though a practicing, apprentice magician will use tools—be they wands, candles, "voodoo" dolls, radionic machines, etc—to help visualize and focus thoughtforms to be projected, a master magician needs no tools other than seasoned, perfected imagination. Many cultures call a person who has reached this level a wizard or witch. I prefer to call practitioners a *Manifestor*, and the most apt a *Master Manifestor*. These are people who create their own reality, whatever that entails, to some degree, each day. Can a Master Manifestor completely create whatever reality he or she wants? Of course not. For that, you would need the biggest mind in the universe. There are always limitations, since the power of your mind is up against the universal mind, or the collective mind of those around you. For example, no matter how proficient you are at manifestation, you will eventually die from the Resistance Layer (or the physical world). This is due to a mind far more powerful than yours alone. What am I talking about? God?

God is not a particular, isolated, sentient being. God is the collective creation. The entire universe is a moving, conscious, active power. Since we are each parts of the collective, whatever abilities you possess are also possessed by the universe. Since you are conscious, the universe is also conscious. Since you move and decide, the universe also moves and decides. The design of the universe is the most efficient design—energies moving via the path of least resistance. That is why characteristics of your cells and atoms (such as orbits) are present and observable in the highest cycles of the universe. Once again, the little represents the big, and the big represents the little. Of course, "little" and "big" are completely relative terms, hence the importance of Einstein's portrayal of relativity in our grasp of how all mechanisms work.

Since the universe is conscious, if you are aware enough, you can perceive the conscious intent, and it will guide you on the most successful, happy course for your life. "Ask and ye shall receive" is grounded in this philosophy. The asking must be sincere, defined, and persistent. The rate of reception is determined by the mind or minds greater than yours, but the request will eventually be fulfilled within those limitations. Since the universe is a creator, and you are a creation, the ability to create is extended within you. You are also a creator. In that sense, the meaning of life is to give life meaning. Every mirror in my house has a piece of paper attached that says "What Will I Create Today?" I suggest you attach such a reminder to every mirror in your house, as well. Over time, you may become a master magician, a *Master Manifestor*.

CHAPTER FOUR

Kukulkan

WHAT YOU have heard about ancient history is mainly hogwash. The history you are given is based on the scientific process. The scientific process can only produce historical conclusions based on fragments that have survived thousands of years. Only a tiny percentage (probably less than one percent) of the information that has been on this earth has lasted through thousands of years. Look around you. How much of what you see will be there in thousands of years?

Interestingly enough, the more advanced a civilization becomes, the less permanent its features become. Just look at the profile we're given by traditional historians. Ancient people carved stuff into stone. When was the last time you carved something into stone? They evolved from stone to papyrus, then paper, each progression becoming less permanent than the last. Priceless libraries have burned to the ground time and time again. Now we hardly even use paper compared to ten years ago. We type things into a digital format (as I'm doing right now) and store it on a flimsy disk or chip. You can leave that medium in the sun for a day, and the information is gone forever. Therefore, you must understand that when we look back at ancient humans, we are only seeing the most primitive representations of their progress. The truly advanced aspects of their cultures left no traces.

Nonetheless, we must work with what we've got. So what can we glean from those heavy stone bits that lasted? One thing is for sure. No matter where you explore on the planet, no matter what culture you investigate, they all say the same thing: We were visited by Gods long ago. Ancients were so adamant about the existence of Gods not because they were stupid and ignorant, but because they WERE being visited. But what do I mean by Gods?

There's no sense in making a fresh case here. Obviously, if you are an ancient person and a flying ship comes down, filled with strange people who have computers, lasers, and such, you can only describe them as superior, divine entities. It is modern historians, in their struggle to define what ancients saw, that are the ones to usually, simply, call them Gods or spirits. I have given you my definition of God. You can also have your own. But for the purpose of reviewing ancient history, we should not apply our terminology. Ancients had interactions with visitors from beyond. Tons of literature has been written on this. So what's new?

It has long been said that, at first, natives could not see the ships of Columbus when he arrived in the New World because of perceptual blindness—inability to see what is not understood. Some have used this as evidence that flying saucers carved in ancient structures could not have been imagined, but reproduced from initial observation. In the discussion of "ancient astronauts," much focus has been placed on the idea the visitors, arriving in these craft, were residents from another rock out there in the cosmos. They somehow advanced enough to overcome the mind-boggling distances and forces to get here. Maybe, on some level, that alone is true. But there is a much, much bigger picture here. And the message those visitors tried to give us has been corroded and corrupted until we were finally ready to understand it; until now . . .

The ancient Maya were truly obsessed with time. You must understand this, and realize it fully. The United States of America has been around over 230 years. The Mayan civilization flourished for 2,250 years. In that amount of time, with their devotion, imagine how much they were able to learn. The Mayan calendar began on the sleepy afternoon of August 11, 3114—a mysterious date completely unrelated to their culture. Yet it ends far after their demise, on Friday, December 21, 2012, when our solar system will align with the center of our galaxy for the first time in recorded history—the first time in 26,000 years. What will happen? I will tell you.

Stories of ancient civilizations being visited by Gods abound. The Maya called their principal God, a visitor from the sky, Kukulkan. The descent of Kukulkan was so long ago, and his wisdom so protected, that we cannot know exactly who he was, or precisely how he engaged the people of earth at that time. He is remembered as a feathered serpent, an inhuman creature, able to fly, who held the powers of destruction and dominance, yet expressed benevolence. Religions and cults devoted to him were widespread and common. Representations of him are preserved and celebrated in architecture across Central and South America.

At Chichen Itza, in the modern Mexican state of Yucatan, the El Castillo pyramid, over 80 feet tall, is devoted to Kukulkan. The long bodies of two stone serpents run down either side of the northern staircase. And on the spring and autumn equinoxes, when the sun is directly above the equator, a shadow forms on the staircase. The shadow looks like the slender, writhing body of a snake. This event is called the Descent of the Feathered Serpent, and it draws a large, celebratory crowd each year.

There are many, varied, stories about Kukulkan. Since I was not there when he visited the people, I cannot tell you with certainty what is true, and what is not, about him. I cannot even say for sure that he ever existed. However, that is not important. I can't tell you with certainty that any ancient deity was here. I can't, with personal first-hand knowledge, tell you about Jesus, or Horus, or Zeuss, or the other 350-some major Gods that one culture or another worshipped. But here's what I can do: I can take them all, from different people, with different languages, spread across this massive planet, and tell you the gist of what most of them said. Because, in a way, majority of the Gods apparently, ultimately said the same thing, hence a singular message that has been passed along by all these unrelated cultures—the only gauge by which we can determine some truth, similar to a policeman separating numerous eyewitnesses to a crime, taking them into different rooms, and questioning them to see if they all come up with the same story. The message of the Gods—the message of Kukulkan—is one that must be looked at from two perspectives. First, we must see it from the time it was given, from the angle of the ancient humans, and then now, from our perspective, looking back after all these years, with all our technology. So why do I single out Kukulkan? It's for a personal reason that I will explain later. But, for now, here is what the ancient Gods were trying to tell us . . . Here is what happened . . .

There has never been a beginning, and there will never be an end. We humans, with our need to move from point to point, chapter to chapter, are preoccupied with our physical births and deaths. We therefore model everything in-between on the concept of start and finish, pacing hour by hour, day by day, week by week, year by year, decade by decade, generation by generation. But that is the product of self-centered, egocentric thinking. Because we are so obsessed with the idea of start and finish, we insist on the idea that there was a beginning to this universe, and there will be an end. But that is not true. This has always been, and will always be. You need not comprehend that. You must overcome the falsehood that humans are capable of grasping everything. Humans are not. Like all beings, humans are capable of understanding exactly what they need at this time, nothing more. You are an infinite part of an infinite world—a great circle—and that is why the measurement of a circle, pi, gives us an infinite number.

The matter in the universe cycles through periods of collision and explosion, like billiard balls bouncing around on a massive table. The infinite table, the horizon of space, never changes; it is a constant medium of swirling energy. In fact, there are tables stacked upon tables, pocket holes connecting them here and there. On our table, long ago, bits of matter congealed into the chunks of rock we call planets.

Earth is not the only planet harboring life. All things are alive. Anything that moves is alive. But earth is special in our neighborhood. It's all Goldilocks indeed—not too hot, not too cold, just right for some wild stuff to happen, at least for now. Why is that so hard to believe? What's so wonderful about all this anyway? It's really chaos, don't you think? It's far less peaceful than those other planets just sitting quietly, still, silent, mature.

There are many out there like it, but this planet is the freak in the neighborhood. Things began to grow here because the conditions were just right. You can dig all day in the dirt, but how often do you pluck out a ruby? How many grains of sand must you toss aside before you find that one anomaly? Imagine each grain of sand is a star or planet, and each ruby is an earth. It's hard to find them, but they're out there, because the conditions were *just right*, and we pay attention to *them*.

The dimensions wobble, going through cycles like everything else. The physical and non-physical change over time. What's physical to you or me today may not be physical to you or me tomorrow. Again, remember that physicality is completely relative. One thing is physical to another if both of them resonate within the same frequency range. If they don't, they pass through each other, like radio waves through your hand. Sometimes, there is a bit of friction though, like microwaves through a potato, and so the potato heats up and bakes. If you became a radio wave, suddenly radio waves would become physical to you, and you could not pass through them. You would be surrounded by huge walls, the radio signals being broadcast from stations all around the earth.

A few thousand years ago, the universe wobbled a bit, and our frequency level increased. Suddenly our planet popped up on the radar of other dimensions. It didn't take long before the visitors arrived. From where did they come and what did they look like? This is a common question.

We know that time is a flexible thing. A clock in your basement runs slower than a clock in your attic, presumably since the earth's gravitational field, stronger near the crust, slows time. Time and space are connected. Therefore, space is flexible. Bearing this in mind, the question "where are they from?" is relative. Where they are from depends on where you are. They may as well be from exactly where you stand, occupying the exact same space you occupy at this moment. Or maybe they are not. It doesn't really matter that much in the long run.

They were advanced enough to know how to get here. That means they were advanced enough to understand how to manipulate matter and energy in whatever way, into whatever form, was necessary for their purposes. In this regard, they could not only come here, but also choose their appearance. They found us hunched, walking on two legs, with two arms. They appeared to us in a variety of ways, usually with two arms and two legs like us. There are some notable exceptions, such as a "burning bush." Do we call them aliens? Interdimensionals? Gods? I prefer to call them *paratemporals*.

Temporality is the way in which you perceive the passing the time, hence the way in, and rate at, which you process information. Your temporal self is the space/time with which you are occupied right now. However, these beings operate outside of that realm, therefore, they are paratemporal. Ghosts, ETs and most cryptids all fit within this definition, since time/space is always warped when they appear. Ghosts are usually a manifestation of the past, thus the distortion of time. When flying saucers appear, people experience missing time. In other cases, a car will stop when a UFO is overhead, but when the craft zips away, the car begins running again, without the ignition being turned once more. This seems to indicate a pause in time, though the human continues to perceive all the while (to be explained later). And in many cases a cryptid, like Bigfoot, is tracked until the footprints just vanish mid-trail. The creature has obviously either de-materialized or been raptured away into the heavens. Either way, it's a manipulation of space which entails a warp of time. The common denominator between most of the entities and phenomena we consider paranormal is their ability to operate beyond your present, temporal perception. "Paratemporal" is a nice, convenient, broad, accurate term for them when referenced in relation to us.

When they came a few thousand years ago, these advanced paratemporal entities saw some great value in our crude lives, and they battled over it, with the same political fervor we engage in today. What did they want from us? They wanted a number of things. Why do we humans fight and try to conquer other lands? When a child asks you "Why did we go to Vietnam?," what is your answer? The quest to take property and dominate others can be explained in many ways, depending on the point of view, but there are always many reasons. One of the things paratemporals wanted was gold.

Beyond mere bartering, the basis of true human currency was exchange of gold. But why have we always considered it so valuable? Of all the substances in our realm, the paratemporals especially wanted the gold. It could be because gold is an excellent electrical conductor that resists corrosion, essential for some of their vehicles and machines. Or it could have been for protection: even today, our astronauts use gold linings in helmets and suits to guard against harmful infrared waves. Gold is so good at reflecting infrared and radio waves, that we also use coatings of it on some satellites, orbiting in space. Plus, gold is so malleable that a single ounce can be beaten into a sheet of 300 square feet, thin enough to bc translucent, yet it remains intact. No traditional historian knows exactly why people have always valued gold so much, and usually says, "mainly because it's *pretty*." But there was something much more. Humans evolved in Africa, where we have found the earliest human remains. The first wave of paratemporals, that wanted gold, encountered humans there, around Babylonia, the cradle of civilization.

In his book, *Rule by Secrecy*, Jim Marrs explores the agenda of the paratemporals. The particular sect he writes about is the Anunnaki, first explored in depth by Zecharia Sitchin. Regarding the question of why the Anunnaki may have wanted gold, Marrs saw fit to quote author Lloyd Pye who, in his book *Everything You Know is Wrong*, wrote: "The Anunnaki sought gold to save their atmosphere, which had apparently sprung leaks similar to those we have created in ours by damaging the Earth's ozone layer . . . The Anunnaki solution was to disperse extremely tiny flakes of gold into their upper atmosphere to patch holes . . . Modern scientists contend that if we are ever forced to repair our own damaged ozone layer, tiny particulates of gold shot into the upper atmosphere would be the best way to go about it."

Regardless of exactly why, the paratemporals wanted to use humans as slaves to mine and shape gold. In the same way our modern scientists play with chimeras and genes, making glow-in-the-dark monkeys, or putting an ear on a mouse's back, the visitors played with our genes. The ultimate goal was to make a hybrid of ancient man and themselves. They wanted a primate with enough strength to work the earth, and enough intelligence to properly handle the complex processes of purifying gold. Hunched, hairy humans changed into something more advanced, made more in the image of the paratemporals, skipping natural stages of evolution by leaps and bounds. "Let us make man in *our* image, after *our* likeness." Gen 1:26.

The modern human served a great purpose for the paratemporals. We were very effective slaves, and to our dominated ancestors, the visitors were truly Gods. When the Spaniards invaded the New World in the 1500s, natives believed the Spanish were immortal. In Puerto Rico, a Taino Indian Chief, and some followers, drowned a Spaniard and watched the corpse for three days to see if it would spring back to life. If the sight of an armored, bearded white man, from a seafaring ship, made such an impression hundreds of years ago, can you imagine how our early modern humans viewed these paratemporals?

The visitors were very well aware of how to herd creatures like humans. They picked certain people as liaisons, individuals with whom they would communicate directly. Those people, perhaps like Moses or Muhammad, would relay messages to larger groups, and have been heralded as prophets and leaders. Because the Gods were associated with gold, idols of gold were often made by cults of humans. And the people were torn over time, as competing divisions of paratemporals battled with each other over the resources of Earth. Each paratemporal considered himself "God" and his competition "the Devil." As always, self-interest, the need to be worshipped and obeyed, was paramount to each one of the visitors.

There were some rogue paratemporals who adopted lives with the humans, even interbreeding with them directly. Many *Bible* scholars might think of those who assimilated into human culture, and tampered with our genes, as the Nephilim. They were considered beings of low caliber by their peers. Most of the paratemporals deemed that behavior unnatural and unbecoming. They condemned it, or at very least, did not condone it.

It was during this time that Kukulkan walked among the ancient Maya. He was solid and physical, as much as you and I are here today. And yet, he was strikingly different. Kukulkan was most likely one of the Nephilim, human-like yet composed of different and bizarre energies. He was impressive, majestic and primordial. Kulkukan was able to fly in some way, move himself through our air and space, gliding smoothly, and so he is figuratively remembered with wings. But he possessed one characteristic that is paramount: he bore shiny, scaly, skin, like a serpent.

Human appearance varies in many ways. Some are tall, some short. We are dark and light, thick and thin, and our eyes and hair take many forms. In saying that Kukulkan looked like a serpent, we don't have to mean he was literally a big snake, but that he resembled a serpent in the same way you might compare a human body type to a particular animal. However, we don't have humans that look serpentine, so he was surely from a different strain of biology; one from elsewhere. Apparently, snakes were the earthly creatures that most resembled this unearthly physiology.

The serpent has always represented mystery and knowledge. In some ways, this knowledge is considered good, in others evil. The most famous example of this is the defining moment in the *Holy Bible*, when Eve first meets Satan's influence in the Garden of Eden. He is manifest as a "serpent," yet not a snake as we know it, since God later punishes the serpent by turning him into the current, slithering form. The reptilian Satanic force persuades Eve to eat from the tree of knowledge, and the serpent tells her, "then your eyes shall be opened, and ye shall be as gods, knowing good and evil" (Genesis 3:5). This alone establishes the Biblical and Christian tradition as one that values ignorance. Knowledge—that thing we so cherish in the modern age—is considered fundamentally evil. The God of the Bible wants us to be ignorant, like pets. Other cultures have considered knowledge good, and thus the reptilian Kukulkan was revered for the wisdom he gave the Maya.

* * *

In May of 2009, I visited the ancient Mayan ruins at Lamanai in Belize. My expedition arrived in the country by ship. We took a long, bumpy ride into the shabby countryside via bus. Next, we sped nearly thirty miles down a dark and twisting river, famous for its crocodiles and monkeys. Eventually, the ruins began to peek from the thick, lush jungle. Lamanai was the most secluded Mayan site, and thrived longer than any other because of this.

It was exhilarating to perch atop towering pyramids, once waterfalls of blood and sacrifice, and turn around completely, breathing in an ancient vista. The jungle teemed with life, and hid tunnels that honeycombed beneath centuries of mud and vines. The ground we walked upon was once rooftop level, the canopy of enormous leaves leaning over us like tired old, arms. Our guide, a Mayan named Carlos, said of the thousands of ruins in Belize, only a handful had been excavated.

In the middle of the site was the ancient ball court. This was perhaps the most sacred place to the ancient Mayans. Unlike today, the ball court was not simply a place for sport, but the grounds upon which sacrifices were determined. The games played in this narrow alley, between two stone walls, would produce winners and losers who would die, live, or be mutilated, based on the outcome. A heavy, 10-pound ball of pure rubber would be heaved around by men using their hips and midsections (no hands and arms allowed) until someone finally knocked it through a stone ring, extending from the alley wall. It was so difficult, that just one score would end the game. Given the sacrificial element, its importance was immense, and the entire affair was done in honor of a visitation long ago—the visitation of beings like Kukulkan.

Though much of the detail is lost, the games were dedicated to the paratemporals who had come. There were various stories about that era. One of them speaks of twin Mayan brothers who were spirited away into the sky to eventually become the sun and the moon. Given the importance of this spot, and its connection to the Gods, I was stunned when I learned what set at its very center—something I had never before heard.

Right in the middle of the court at Lamanai, an obvious obstacle for those men feverishly playing the game, was a circular stone, perhaps the size of a hoola-hoop. It was about one foot thick. All in all, it looked like a large ancient wheel, but it was not. This was actually a capstone. In the 1980s, archaeologists lifted it and found it sealed an ancient time capsule. Within were a few clay containers. The centerpiece was a cylinder filled with 131 grams of liquid mercury.

To this day, archaeologists are not sure where the ancient Maya obtained liquid mercury, nor why it was given such a place of prominence. The best speculation was that it had somehow been refined from cinnabar deposits in Guatemala and brought over; in fact, containers of cinnabar, jade, and obsidian were found in the chamber, as well. Modern Maya know stories of ancient shaman who would gain sinister power by placing a drop of mercury in their veins. If lucky enough to survive death by poisoning, the shaman came close to the nether realm, absorbing its dark magic. This may be true, yet the placement of the liquid mercury immediately struck a deeper chord with me.

The German Nazis spent much time in Central and South America in the 1930s and 40s, even constructing secret compounds in South America. Teams of scientists studied weird ancient knowledge, reinterpreting it in the language of modern physics. The Nazis clearly believed ancient cultures incorporated, or were at least exposed to, super-advanced technology, but lacked the understanding to properly document the forces at work. For a while, the German tech may have been so advanced because they took metaphysical archaeology seriously, and recreated elements they discovered at lost sites. Records of exactly what the Nazis found are scarce, but some of their most secret compounds were in Mayan territory.

Many fine researchers of obscure Nazi war plans, like Joseph P. Farrell and Jim Marrs, have found records of the single weapon most coveted by the Germans. It was called Die Glocke, or "The Bell." This was a metal case, 9 feet wide and 12 to 15 feet high, roughly shaped like a bell, that housed two counter-rotating cylinders filled with a substance similar to *liquid mercury.* When the cylinders spun, time and space around the device were warped, and the entire machine actually lost weight, floating into the air. The Nazis were working on an anti-gravity device that also produced deadly radiation. The military potential was truly unlimited.

It is interesting to note that the Mayan calendar, such a mantle of debate, is not a stationary stone engraved with symbols. It is a dynamic machine, and consists of two *counter-rotating* disks, with a smaller third disk included, as well. Together, these three disks function like cogged wheels of clockwork, aligning three symbols that can be interpreted in various ways. We'll dig into the calendar more later, but note the potential connection here between the Mayan focus on liquid mercury and counter-rotating machinery, and the Nazis usage of a liquid-mercury-type substance in a counter-rotating device as their possible ultimate weapon, or *Wunderwaffe*.

The Nazis supposedly achieved anti-gravity in a bell-shaped (saucer-like) metal craft. The Maya placed their liquid mercury in the center of a site that revered extraterrestrial/inter-dimensional visitation. It seems quite plausible that the Nazis learned much from the ancient Maya about how the paratemporal craft functioned. As I investigated deeper, I found strange deposits of liquid mercury had also been discovered at other notable sites of mystery, like the pyramids in Egypt and China. The ancient Vedic literature of India speaks in great detail of Vimana, strange, ET flying machines powered by engines of whirling mercury. All the pieces had fallen into place.

CHAPTER FIVE
Wisdom & Time

KUKULKAN and the paratemporals—what some call Nephilim—did not travel in cars, or by horseback. They flew in the liquid mercury machines, or "Quick Silvers." Though found on earth, the heart of the device, the mercury, appeared so foreign to the Maya, just as it still does to us today, that they revered it and its mystical properties. And yet, the Quick Silvers were not just rigid, metal frames, as we so often think of UFOs today. As they spun and warped time, their energy fields became less fluid.

When you put your hand on a video game joystick and apply pressure, that pressure creates electrical signals. Those electrical signals travel through fine conduits to affect change. If that joystick is attached to the wheels of a tank, the wheels spin and you move forward. This is just one way of transferring your conscious desire to a vehicle. The paratemporals were so advanced they had transcended that stage. Their vehicles were conscious-sensitive. Hands placed on controls could directly guide the Quick Silvers. Furthermore, as our modern science of understanding consciousness evolves, it seems the craft may not have simply been steered with thoughts, but actually *powered* by thoughts, as well. These craft were a mesh of organic and inorganic materials. Outwardly, the sleek shell could function aerodynamically, while inwardly, components were actually living, able to sense and transfer bio-energy effortlessly.

The Quick Silvers were made of a consciousness-sensitive material, with a spinning mercury core. Because of this, the craft could change form depending on the conditions within which it functioned. In earth's atmosphere, a reflective saucer-shape worked well, under the water, perhaps a sphere, in outer space, a high-energy blaze of plasma. The machine adapted to its environment. But because the Quick Silvers were sensitive to consciousness, a force also directed by humans, the human observers themselves could, and always have, literally influenced the form of the machines. That is why, throughout history, UFO reports have often reflected the expectations of the witnesses, an even stronger effect when in the presence of a large group of humans, willfully shaping the experience—manifesting what they expect and hope to see.

The humans surrounding Kukulkan did not even understand how a simple airplane worked. How was he to explain to them, in great detail, the workings of the Quick Silvers? These were simply magic to the Maya, and Kukulkan was the great magician. Most of the humans were illiterate, and there was no mass media for mass communication. Therefore, Kukulkan could only seriously explain himself to a select few, allowed to surround him. The Maya were extremely intelligent, yet extremely barbaric. This may seem difficult to understand, but it can be said of all successful civilizations. Cultures are composed of many layers of human understanding, and only those that possess factions brutal enough to conduct merciless war have survived and flourished so that some of their records exist even today. We can fault the Maya for their violent society and superstitions, yet is the world so different today? As I write these words, the globe is still embroiled in religious wars, fought in the name of superstitions and imaginary beings, even as we call ourselves civilized and great. The Mayan histories record Kukulkan as a benevolent God who could have destroyed everyone, but did not. It may not be entirely accurate to call him good or bad. He was, as usual, simply self-serving. But because he did not take sport in maliciously causing pain and suffering, and preferred to see humans work together in productive cooperation, he is a beloved figure to this day. Maybe a fundamental Christian who could see those days in a crystal ball would call him The Devil since he did influence the people and he left them with knowledge. Perhaps Kukulkan would call the Christian God The Devil, having successfully deceived the world by reversing roles. There really is no Devil, though, just man's animalistic tendency to be greedy and selfish. That urge may never die, and if knowledge feeds it, so be it. Regardless, Kukulkan did give us wisdom.

Kukulkan, the Serpent God, explained to the Mayan priests how the Quick Silvers could warp space and time. He was from another place, but more importantly, another dimension; one that vibrated at a faster rate than ours. He tried to explain how his craft would change forms as it altered dimensions and conditions, protecting the pilot, and adapting almost instantly to its environment. He explained that they travel because they can, and because they need resources like all beings, and our world is rich. But perhaps most importantly, Kukulkan told them of the cosmic breath.

The cosmic breath is the rhythmic ebb and flow of the universe. The galaxies undulate, expanding and contracting like a massive breast, coming and going like seasons, with one cycle taking many thousands of years. And just as the temperature rises and falls on earth as seasons change, the frequencies of the universe rise and fall as the cycles come and go. Once every few thousand years, the frequency level of our earth is raised, and suddenly we appear on the "radar" of those other dimensions, usually invisible to us. There is a convergence of our dimensions. The two do not completely overlap, but come close enough together so that, using the Quick Silvers, more paratemporals are able to visit us. Some can visit us at any time, and there are miniature convergences, or "flaps" from time to time, but the increase around the mass convergence is so great that the other times pale in comparison.

Kukulkan was there in the midst of a cosmic convergence. The world was filled with paratemporals like him then. He explained how humans could predict these convergences by watching the stars, identifying the cycles of heavenly bodies, and see their patterns reflect frequency and vibrational change. The Mayan obsession with time, dedication to the great calendar, was solidified. He told them that the mass convergence in which they sat would end soon, and he, and most of his kind, would fade away, first zipping away in their Quick Silvers. But those like him, perhaps even himself depending on how time passed, would come back during the next mass convergence, a new chapter. It would begin around December 21, 2012.

So what did he say would happen in 2012? Would it be like someone had flipped a switch and the world would turn upside down? No. It would be the start of a gradual shift in human perception, allowing us to experience the paratemporals once again with greater regularity. These experiences would open the minds of humans, and show them the wisdom of working together, overcoming many of the petty divisions within the human race that divide us now. In the words of President Ronald Reagan, "I occasionally think how quickly our differences worldwide would vanish if we were facing an alien threat from outside this world. And yet, I ask, is not an alien force ALREADY among us?"

Yes, December 21, 2012 will be marked by an alignment of our galaxy with the solar system, the likes of which has not been since in around 26,000 years. And yes, researchers like Terrence McKenna, having compared history with the I Ching, have made a fascinating case for how the historical "time wave" of events might break down on that particular day, condensing into something unknown. The I Ching itself is based on the idea that tossed coins fall in certain patterns because they simply represent a miniature model of greater forces in the universe, and can be read to help determine aspects of your fate. Those are mesmerizing topics to be dwelled upon. But they are simply indicators of the great dimensional convergence. Once begun, human minds will open for the next 1000 years, as humans are exposed to mysterious interactions on a scale not seen in centuries. This is the meaning, and purpose, and hope for a new era of human enlightenment, risen from the ashes of the old, ignorant ways that have built on the misinterpreted fragments of the last great convergence. Destruction of the old is necessary for fresh growth, and that transition will be traumatic. So will anything happen to you on December 21, 2012, at 11:11 UT? You will most likely feel a tiny pinprick between your eyes. This will be the opening of the third eye, and a new perception. Then you may be light headed.

* * *

As the global frequency changed with cosmic nature, the vast majority of the paratemporals—"angels" and "demons"—slowly faded from our dimension after the great convergence. Some have been able to pop in and out ever since, especially during mini-convergences, like the year 1947 or the period from 1964-1968. All the while, the promise was that a return would occur in the distant future; beginning in 2012.

Our history is scattered and inconsistent. The written records are filled with vague references to giant skeletons, often horned, that have been uncovered in places like Pennsylvania or North Carolina, only to mysteriously vanish or simply fall from documentation (see *Pet Ghosts*). There are also stone monuments bearing weird petroglyphs never understood, such as Judaculla Rock in Cullowhee, North Carolina. We can't be sure how many of these are connected to underground cultures or periodic visits from paratemporal beings. But we can feel confident, in some scattered fashion, beings from other realms have continued to influence the shape of our human development.

Through the years, those who came into personal contact with the most impressive paratemporals used their privileged knowledge and experiences to dominate their peers, just as the paratemporals dominated all humankind. And some of them have indeed apparently stayed in contact to some extent. They know that no matter what powers humans create, the visitors can outdo it, and so that relationship is held in the highest regard for security and dominance. Those with this contact, and the heirs of those with this contact, have used it to influence the affairs of their lives, gain wealth and strength—give themselves *an edge*. And this is the great secret kept by our rulers in the modern society. But I'm not talking about mere presidents and political figureheads.

Our world is controlled by money. The paratemporals set the gold standard for that money long ago. And so, no matter how eloquent, sincere, or persuasive a speaker, transforming thoughts and words into action requires money. Not only is it necessary to provide our basic survival needs, but a person can be imprisoned for not paying a tax imposed by his fellows. The people who run for high office require millions of dollars to succeed; truly astronomical sums that automatically separate "them" from "us" the commoners. If you were to give a politician a great sum of money, you'd want to make sure you could somehow control that politician. Blackmail is a common tool, and thus we fill our offices with "blackmailable" people who are naturally corruptible in order to simply be a legitimate candidate. That is why politics is incessantly rocked with scandals as glimpses of that corruption inevitably peek out.

Your money comes from a bank. And that bank's money comes from a bigger bank. And that bank's from an even bigger one. And as you go higher and higher up the food chain you eventually find that there is one ultimate bank to which all roads in the modern banking industry leads: The Bank for International Settlements in Basel, Switzerland. It stands as a dark tower, like Mount Doom. There are around 20 public directors, reps from various "civilized" countries like the U.S. (head man of the Federal Reserve), London, Tokyo, etc. And there is a private group of owners. These are the people who directly control the world.

One of Bill Clinton's mentors, Carroll Quigley, wrote in his book, *Tragedy and Hope: A History of the World in Our Time (1966)*:

"...the powers of financial capitalism had another far-reaching aim, nothing less than to create a world system of financial control in private hands able to dominate the political system of each country and the economy of the world as a whole. This system was to be controlled in a feudalist fashion by the central banks of the world acting in concert, by secret agreements arrived at in frequent private meetings and conferences. The apex of the system was to be the Bank for International Settlements in Basle, Switzerland, a private bank owned and controlled by the world's central banks which were themselves private corporations."

Those people who privately make decisions at the highest financial levels are the heirs of those who have secretly protected the knowledge of the paratemporal visitations, both long ago, and even today. These connections have been traced and documented well by a number of conspiracy researchers including David Icke and Alex Jones. The material is not hard to find if one is willing to look for it.

There are many ignorant people who immediately roll their eyes and scoff at the idea of "conspiracy." These people represent the dumbest of our peers. Each day, around the world, people are imprisoned on charges of criminal conspiracy. A conspiracy begins the moment one person says to another, "let's just keep this between the two of us." It isn't necessarily some vast, incredible, intricate plan that is concealed. However, even those are known to succeed. If you have any doubt that thousands of people can work in concert to keep a secret, just look at the Manhattan Project or Allied operation for D-Day in WW2.

Every organization, be it a family or a business, is filled with private information, and sly ways of wording things to preserve the privacy of the organization. And yes, the natural model for organization is the pyramid, with a few ambitious, strong folks at the top and an ever-expanding mass of less informed supporters beneath, working only at what they alone need; never able to, or allowed to, observe the big picture. "Conspiracy" is a rather sinister word for an element of basic human psychology, and certainly does not need further justification.

The truly ironic part is that secrecy really doesn't exist! People have big mouths, and gossip about things before thinking about the repercussions of doing so. Of course we always have deathbed confessions, during which very few powers can restrain one's will to speak the truth. All of the truth is all around you—in books, on the internet, presented by passionate speakers at conferences. But the trick is knowing which ones to believe. THAT is, has always been, and will always be, the method by which the truth is concealed. Those who want to conceal something don't simply lie about it. They foster 10 different versions of the truth. The average person quickly becomes frustrated and exhausted by exploring each one and gives up on the entire exercise. That is why the vast majority of the public enables the conspiracy to function perpetually. Most of us are lazy, unmotivated and, most of all, distracted. And a system that makes you work like a dog to survive ensures that you remain distracted most of the hours in your busy day. And one more thing: people are also afraid. They fear going to hell, or disappointing their parents and teachers, or doctors and pastors, or being looked down upon by the neighbors or employers or co-workers, mainly because of low self-esteem and overwhelming self-deception and hypocrisy. Do not cower before religious leaders, family members, educators, arrogant scientists, politicians, etc, who call you crazy for your open mind and deeper understanding of the apparent. Do not continue to enable your own mental slavery by those who are often falsely considered well-educated, yet are actually the most ignorant and hostile among us. Only your intolerance can eventually improve the world for everyone!

And so those who are fortunate enough to descend from those who originally held court with the paratemporals are now those who call the shots, deciding war and peace, setting tones for customs and etiquette, tools they can use to make themselves look and sound superior to everyone else—a mind game to the end. In a way, they are our representatives of the ancient visitors; their ambassadors and prophets. And we conquer other lands for the same reasons the Gods conquered us: self-interest.

Descendants of the prophets have always worked together through their own private systems, their secret societies. I won't use any particular names here since they carry so much baggage. Besides, if you know the name of the secret society it's not nearly so secret as those whose names remain hidden. But today, just how closely aligned are the human powers with those Gods? Are some people actually shape-shifting reptilians that feed on human blood? If this is true, it's the easiest secret to keep in the world—no one would ever believe it! Could there be entities from beyond that feast upon us. Why not? Probably. The world is larger and more complex than we can possibly imagine. Are we food for someone else? Each year, millions of people around the planet simply vanish without a trace. Never forget: I bet there is not one single cow on this earth that knows people eat cows. Why should we know if we are being digested by something superior, if not physically, then directly by our energy. After all, the only reason to eat a plant or animal is so it will dissolve and ultimately give you its energy. Some life forms in the universe have probably evolved to surpass the eating of the physical flesh, going straight for the energy, the end product. In fact, humans seem to have this ability, as well. Some people always drain your energy—psychic vampires—while others fill you with electricity and excitement.

No two people see the world the same way. An obvious example may be two guys sitting in a bar. One sees a woman and finds her attractive. The other sees the woman and does not. Whose perception is correct? Obviously, there is no correct perception, only different ones. Each man is seeing something different, and only that man can ever truly know what he sees. In this regard, we are completely alone and isolated within our own senses, doomed to only know the world around us a particular way. In this regard, I think some people are able to look at another human and decode what they see in a special way. They might observe that person's reptilian energy field. In the same way, if a ghost passed through a room, perhaps one would see it while others did not. Some people are apparently able to spot those who are closer to the genes of our ancestors like Kukulkan. Maybe we all shape-shift into various fields all the time, but only some are sensitive and perceptive enough to see it. The reptilian field is especially strong, though.

The secret contact with paratemporals is really not so secret. It's just not fully divulged by official government sources. It is somewhat puzzling that humans are so dependent on the façade of government that they *need* officials to acknowledge something. Why do you insist on believing there are people smarter than you? If you walk outside and see a UFO or a ghost, who gives a damn what the government says? Believe your experience. That is all you have.

Governments are in the business of keeping secrets. That is the key to maintaining an upper hand. Even the descendents of the paratemporals fight among themselves, competing for the favor of the Gods to this day. I have no doubt there are bases on the moon, and have been for some while. We didn't go there just to put on a big, expensive show. Satellites are the unblinking eyes in the sky. Look at how much our lives revolve around man-made satellites, and imagine just how valuable control of the moon, the ultimate satellite, has always been. If you view a clear night sky with Generation III Night Vision Goggles (especially the ones available at www.Paratemporal.com), you will see all kinds of strange things flying around on the edge of space that are not satellites or space junk. Using Night Vision, I observed an enormous v-shaped formation, in February of 2009, flying at night over the desert of Laughlin, Nevada (I was speaking at the International UFO

Congress). Our world governments surely have an advanced space program that is hidden, perhaps even integrating paratemporals.

Years ago, I presented the world with a video clip (given to me by the late Charles Yost) that showed what appeared to be a smokestack jutting from the lunar surface, with a cloud jettisoned from the top. Instantly, and for months, my associates and I were harassed by a counter-intelligence operation that worked inexhaustibly around the clock to dispute any information posted, no matter how speculative, right or wrong. Who were these people? They were the spooks behind the spooks—the public relations arm of "the descendants" who specialize in targeting and squashing any information that seems to come out from a half-way credible source. The leading world governments have divisions interested in all paranormal phenomena, especially because paranormal events often occur in conjunction with the production of plasma, the fourth state of matter. Plasma has immense applications for weaponry, communications, transportation, shielding, and propulsion—as Nikola Tesla knew.

Have you noticed the incredible amount of UFO video footage that comes from Mexico? Why should a relatively poor country produce more video of this sort than the United States or Japan where video cameras are more plentiful? Obviously, it's because there is more activity there. But why? It's because, for years, the United States military has produced weird, top-secret experiments in Mexico. People in the United States don't keep up with what's happening in Mexico—most of them don't even speak the language. And it's cheap to work down there. This is why the U.S. government has been so tolerant of illegal aliens coming across the border from Mexico (until they use it as an excuse for a new form of electronic I.D. and global currency coming for everyone). Behind the scenes, the U.S. military and Mexican military have a mutually-beneficial relationship. And if something goes haywire and destroys half a Mexican state, there won't be as much flack as if half of Nevada vanished. Of course, considering much of Kukulkan's activity was around Mexico and Central

America, activity there may be picking up as we head toward, and through, 2012, since Kukulkan's culture might plan to visit the same location again. Even huge flying serpents, slithering in the sky, are being reported and videotaped there. Could the serpent-like reptilians of Kukulkan also have been related to ancient dragons, and the terrifying, yet regal, treatment of dragon symbology across the globe?

Weapons experimentation draws attention from paratemporals. There are many examples of craft interfering with bases and military operations. But perhaps the best example is the Roswell incident. The first modern nuclear explosions occurred in New Mexico. The atomic bombs dropped on Hiroshima and Nagasaki were delivered from the Roswell base. It was a top secret facility, full of the world's best aviators (insulted when told they were only seeing weather balloon debris). Less than two years after the nukes were dropped, this UFO crashed near Roswell. That same month, around 20 days later, President Truman signed the National Security Act, forming the Air Force and CIA, and laying the grounds for the NSA. Coincidence?

Some conspiracy experts, like celebrated aviator John Lear, feel confident that earthly governments work with aliens to experiment on humans in dark, horrific ways. Stories about underground alien bases in Dulce, New Mexico, or even at Brown Mountain, give us pause. If unethical and downright horrible things are being done to citizens in the name of national security, it makes sense for much of it to be done in, or near, Mexico, where accountability is minimized. At various places around the country, like Taos, New Mexico, entire populations complain of being driven half-mad by a constant, low rumbling, like the hum of machinery, below the ground. Just how extensive are these underground bases?

I should also mention that new information on Roswell continues to surface. Researcher David Sereda videotaped an interview with Boyd Bushman, a senior scientist at Lockheed

Martin for years. Bushman claims he knew the pilot who "shot down" the Roswell craft using a secret weapon (that Sereda thinks may have been based on Tesla's work). According the Bushman, the pilot got the opportunity to walk inside the downed craft. He said the outside shined metallic, but once inside, he could see out through transparent walls (similar to one-way glass). He also said the floor was spongy, and that the creatures were half organic and half inorganic. Bushman was so inspired by the alien tech, that he produced a simple anti-gravity experiment. He bolted two powerful neodymium magnets together (forcing them against their opposing fields) and dropped them repeatedly from a 59-foot tower, reproducing Galileo's famous gravity experiment. The magnet apparatus would consistently hit the ground later than a control. This defied physical laws, proving an anti-gravity effect somehow based on magnetic stress. Bushman said nine scientists signed an affidavit confirming they had witnessed this over and over. Is a wonderful key to our knowledge, even this simple, being selfishly hoarded by government scientists to this day?

Government is a ruthless business that takes full advantage of public weakness. And institutions that reflect the same organizational model, like many churches and schools, are no different. I have been criticized for "believing in" ghosts by people who, in the same breath, pray to a God! How are the concepts of ghosts and paratemporals any less believable than the idea of God, angels, demons, and other spiritual presences? Some people are so self-unaware that they can't even separate themselves from their personal experiences. If they grew up with it, it's normal to them—no matter how weird to anyone else. Oddly enough, most people are oblivious to their own self-contradictory views. Those who seek to control (and that's what people in the government actually do) will use the confused minds of the masses and twist those strange thoughts into whatever serves the controller best. It's all mind control on one level or another. If we are to view the world by strict scientific standards, religion of any sort seems inherently insane.

Thomas Jefferson was roundly criticized for saying "It does me no injury for my neighbor to say there are 20 Gods or no God. It neither picks my pocket nor breaks my leg." That is the approach we should use in all government. There should be a difference between one's personal morals and ethics and that common ground of legislation upon which we must all agree to behave. Mind your own business. And as long as you don't harm someone else directly, do whatever you like. My campaign slogan would be privacy, prosperity and personal freedom. Little changes could be done to help restore pure leadership again. We should require no bill to be longer than ten pages so our representatives *might* actually have a chance to read it. And every law should expire after ten years. If it's not important enough to renew in ten years, we probably don't need it!

The simplest form of passive aggressive ridicule that stifles paranormal exploration is one person responding to another with this old phrase: "it's probably just your imagination." This is actually an insult, said to a person who is being lightly accused of an inability to separate what is important from what is not. It is true that we sometimes completely generate things from within, therefore imagining them. But we should never discount something out of hand because it *might* be imagined. Maybe the reason it was generated within is that it is a response to something outside. But that level of thoughtfulness is scarcely applied by most in our society. We should stop saying "it could be your imagination" unless we intend to degrade someone. Though that kind of soft mind control has always been used, our technology now confronts us with hard-core mind reading machines. Functional magnetic resonance imaging (or fMRI) is a system of mapping the brain with such intricacy that specific words and thoughts can be extracted from the mind. In 2009, the *60 Minutes* news program did a detailed segment on the technology, demonstrating its successful operation and explaining how it can be used for criminal and terrorist prosecution in the very near future. Will potential intention one day be upheld as evidence of wrongdoing, as presented in Spielberg's 2002 movie *Minority Report*?

It's sad to see the system of distraction and mass mind control has been so effective. Much of today's youth lives in a cyber world and depends on it. And yet that world is so fragile that it could collapse at any moment. Would they know how to repair it? My friend Bill Forstchen wrote a best-selling novel called *One Second After*. It's about an electromagnetic pulse (or EMP) that blasts the United States from a nuke that is detonated miles above. Instantly, most of the country reverts back to the pioneer days. In the novel, looting and chaos ensue, and those who know how to survive take over. That scenario is so real that Bill has been contacted by military leaders and Congressional committees asking him to speak before them and fully explain the implications of this threat.

On September 1, 1859, an amazing episode, known as the Carrington Event, occurred. An English solar astronomer named Richard Carrington observed a bright spot on the sun that rapidly swelled, then dwindled, at 11:18am. Five minutes later, the skies of earth brightened into brilliant, colorful auroras. Telegraph lines went nuts, shooting sparks that caught office papers on fire. An enormous solar flare had induced powerful electrical currents through all metal on earth. In a 1962 test called Starfish Prime, the United States detonated a large nuclear device 250 miles above the Pacific Ocean. Almost 1000 miles away, in Hawaii, the EMP it produced destroyed 300 streetlights, fused power lines, and took out telephones, televisions, radios, and burglar alarms. With today's world so dependent on sensitive electronics, can you imagine what a powerful EMP, either natural or from enemy attack, could do? Interestingly, many solar scientists think, due to massive sun activity, our next best chance for a possible Carrington-type EMP event will be 2012. When you have a virus, your body runs a fever. Some, like the Lakota Indians, say humans are now a virus on earth, and mother nature will eventually heat up to destroy us, too.

But for now, all continues in the manmade architecture of control. The world is controlled by money. The money is controlled by descendents of those who knew the paratemporals. Therefore, the greatest secret being kept by human civilization is the wisdom and power of the paratemporals. But what exactly is the power of the paratemporals? What is it that is so important to them? Simple: the ability to warp space-time. Time is of particular interest, hence the *Paratemporal Loop Hypothesis*.

CHAPTER SIX

The Paratemporal Loop Hypothesis

A HYPOTHESIS is an explanation or model that hinges on at least one testable element. If that element eventually tests in favor of the hypothesis, it then becomes a theory. In this case, the one condition that is testable is whether or not traveling into the past is possible. If ever, (ever, ever, ever in the infinite future!) under any circumstances, humans or similar beings figure out how to travel back in time, we can suppose they *will*. This is the basis of the Paratemporal Loop Hypothesis.

Just to be extreme, let us imagine that millions of years into the future, after humans are long gone, another species, based on mammals, reptiles, amphibians, birds, insects, fish, or some type of life yet unknown, advances and surpasses our present human state and becomes the first to figure out how to travel back in time. Even if it is illegal to do so, a rogue scientist won't be able to resist the temptation. For the sake of example, let's say the first person is Fishman, a highly evolved humanoid from the earth's ocean.

Fishman travels back to the year 1920. We view time as an inexorable march ever forward, based on our perception. But in going back, even while his timeline continues, Fishman has now created a time loop—one we will call a paratemporal loop. He knows how important it is for him to remain hidden and elusive. If he makes too big an impact on the world, especially if he is seen, he could affect the chain of events ever after and jeopardize his own future existence. As a result, he would fade away like the lead character in *Back to the Future*. However, if Fishman is willing to take a risk, he could try to create some result that might enhance his position in the future. Let's say Fishman brings back a disease that will wipe out the genes of his future predator. If the risk has been calculated correctly, he may return to a better future. If he fails, he may either vanish or his future could be worse. But Fishman says what the heck and gives it a try. If he fails, then it's over, and who knows when the next being will travel back? But if it succeeds, then Fishman is now stronger when he returns, and he ruthlessly protects the time travel technology so that no one can go back and mess him up. Let's say he successfully keeps this secret for a few years, then he wakes up one day and world has changed somehow. He's confused. How did this happen?

What Fishman didn't realize was that in a million years after he was born, long after Fishman is gone, Bearman (who has evolved from the future forests) discovers how to travel back, and he has done the same thing as Fishman, traveling to 1915, five years before Fishman went back, tweaking the past to his advantage. So now Fishman has to go back again, this time to 1914, and correct it to his liking. He is now engaged in a sort of time battle with Bearman. But what neither Fishman nor Bearman realize is that in all of the future, there are thousands of others, just like them. What we therefore have is a very complex series of millions of paratemporal loops, with countless members of countless future species all trying to outdo each other in favor of their own personal self interests in the future. And they are not fully aware of each other. What a mess! So, how does this affect you and me in our lives?

What if the world around you actually does change somehow from day to day, hour to hour, or second to second, as you move through this intricate structure of loops, some lasting days, some lasting less than a second? One moment flying saucers exist; the next moment they don't. One moment Bigfoot exists; the next moment, he does not. Have you ever sworn you saw a detailed news feature about a celebrity who had died? Then you find out later that the celebrity is alive again? This is called the "dead celebrities phenomenon" and may actually occur with many people, but we simply notice celebrities more since they are famous. Can other people vanish and reappear without any awareness of what has happened to them? Read about the 1890 Thunderbird Photo from Tombstone, Arizona, in my book *Pet Ghosts*. Thousands of people around the world swear they have seen it, yet no one can produce a copy. Where did it go? Was it removed from our current timeline by someone? Are we passing through an ever-changing world, fluid in ways beyond our comprehension, constantly tweaked in a multi-faceted tug of war by beings in the future? And yes, some of them may be humans. What if humans actually figured out how to do this long ago, but it has been kept secret from most of us? What if members of the human race are actively playing this game as we speak?

It all sounds like some dizzying plot in a bad sci-fi movie and yet, if the premise of the Hypothesis, which is very plausible, is true, then this is surely the realistic outcome. The one thing that most paranormal entities have in common is a connection to warped time. As touched on earlier, remember that ghosts usually represent a glimpse of the past, or a person as they appeared in the past. A UFO hovers above a car and the vehicle stops. When the UFO zips away, the vehicle starts running again, even though the ignition was not turned. The car didn't die, so time was apparently stopped. Someone follows Bigfoot, leaving behind a trail of tracks, then suddenly the tracks stop in mid-trail and the creature is gone. The Bigfoot has warped its place in space, and since space-time is a single element, in changing space, the creature's time is also changed. And yet you may ask, if a UFO hovers above and a car stops because time stands still, why doesn't it make the driver freeze, as well? Of course, in some cases, this does account for the "missing time" reported by witnesses. But in other cases, the human mind continues to function because the mind is, itself, a time machine that generally functions independently. When you remember what you had for lunch yesterday, you are mentally traveling through time. When you imagine the outcome of tomorrow's election, you are traveling into a future possible timeline.

Some people experience paranormal activity all the time. Others never experience it at all. Why is this? It may be because everyone has a unique brain, and therefore a unique time machine. You actually have an entire life path that is aligned with your own pattern of loop perception. The loops around us, in their layers, create frequencies. Some people have a brain tuned to the frequency of the UFO realm, and others do not. This goes for any phenomenon. Just as the length of an antenna can determine what electromagnetic signals one can detect, variables within your brain and mind can determine what aspects of reality you are most apt to receive. In this sense, our worlds overlap somewhat, but we each are truly experiencing a unique reality—the product of our own personal interface with the web of timelines we encounter each day, each timeline full of new, yet fleeting, possibilities. In some of them you may be psychic. In others, you are not. Your ability can come and go second by second or year by year.

When, on your conscious journey through life, you pass through a substantial specific point where a loop has connected, time at that spot ceases to exist as we usually experience it. At that point, we are sometimes able to more easily perceive phenomena that are suspended in time; especially ghosts, be them conscious or imprints. Also at the joints, our potential for ESP is enhanced, allowing the time machine of your mind easier access to stretch into the past or future. It is highly possible that even if the staple of the Paratemporal Loop is wrong, and beings have never been, nor will ever be, capable of traveling through time, similar time loops may exist naturally, as well.

Humans represent the passing of time in a straightforward, linear fashion. A common modern calendar is laid out in a line of Monday, Tuesday, Wednesday, etc. We therefore imagine ourselves moving straight ahead in a smooth procession. But what if this model does not correspond to the genuine shape of time? Just one little twist here and there can turn everything upside down. If you take a strip of paper, twist it one time, then tape the ends together, you have something similar to a figure eight. If you then place the tip of a pen in the middle of the strip and never lift the tip as you draw straight forward, you will eventually find that you come back to the place where you started. Then if you undo the ends, you will find that although you never lifted the pen, you actually drew a straight line down the middle of both sides. If you were an ant crawling straight forward on that strip, you never would have realized that you shifted over to the other side and back. This design is called a *Mobius Strip.*

Often, just before someone witnesses a paranormal event, they describe, in retrospect, an eerie moment of silence just before the manifestation. It seems as if time almost stops for a moment, and the individual is utterly alone. And then—POW—the weirdness happens. English researcher Jenny Randles calls this The Oz Factor, a sign that one is about to cross into a new realm. If time is occasionally shaped like a Mobius strip, maybe sometimes you encounter one of these twists in the timeline. That moment, just before you switch over to the other realm, all is quiet because you are not quite here nor there. You are in some fuzzy purgatory for a few seconds, devoid of the usual sensory input. And when you return back to the other side of this timeline Mobius strip, you are left dazed by how "out of place" and unreal the entire experience seemed.

In some cases, for a while, you may even continue to simultaneously exist in two timelines. Has someone ever seen you somewhere you have never been, doing something that you did not do? Some people even run into themselves—face to face with their doppelganger or double. Modern physicists have photographed the same particle at two separate places at the same time. Though we cannot comprehend this, it happens, and it may occur in our lives from time to time.

As you have read thus far, our world, filled with mystery, is complex enough when simply viewed from one point of view. But now, imagine that complexity multiplied exponentially, as those phenomena are also occurring within these countless paratemporal loops. The enormous range of subtle frequencies that waver and fluctuate, bringing us in and out of contact with a mind-boggling spectrum of energies and beings operates within an everchanging reality, shifting ever so slightly, like waves of light on a hot road, as forces from the future struggle with those in the past to determine those possible futures again and again.

In some loops, we experience the flying humanoids, like Mothman. Such winged beings exist just beyond our normal, physical vibration. And when there is a large, impending change in our world on the physical level, it is preceded by a gradual and powerful change in the energy environment. Like electrical charges building in a capacitor, they strengthen, and warp our dimensions, bringing us into contact with those beings, seemingly omens of transformation. And then, when finally the physical change occurs, often quickly and violently, all the energies snap back into place, removing those beings from our realm until another convergence can occur. Perhaps winged beings sometimes blast into our dimension with such force that they accidentally destroy themselves. The incredible Tunguska explosion of 1908 left a huge, butterfly-like blast pattern on the ground, considered unexplained to this day.

Many of the creatures so popular in paranormal lore—bigfoot, aliens, mothmen, ghosts, chupacabra, so-called angels and demons—are glimpsed when the dimensions warp toward each other once in a while. During that limited interaction, most of the parties are somewhat confused, especially those I call phantimals; paratemporals that appear more animal-like than human-like (again, read *Pet Ghosts*). In many cases, our ability to see and interact with them is just as surprising to us as their ability to see and interact with us is to them. And yet, some of them appear to truly understand what is going on.

It seems rather likely that future humans do in fact figure out how to travel into the past. They may not be fully organic like us, though. Because we think of ourselves as organic, we are organo-centric beings. But you are composed of metal, as well. When spilled, your blood leaves iron rust. As we advance, we will surely become more like cyborgs, blurring the line between the current concept of man and machine. It's already happening. How often do you see someone with a tiny cell phone/computer practically glued to the ear? In the future, we will be a combination of organic and inorganic, just like the advanced ships of the paratemporals. That is why some describe such qualities of grays, and also why there is something so unsettling inhuman about the Men in Black (or MIB).

If you want to understand the MIB, you must ask yourself one very simple question: why, especially throughout the 20th century, did these men always dress in black? It is now so well known that it seems they would stick out like sore thumbs. And, because of that, we don't hear as many reports of them. For the most part, they have apparently changed their dress. But why? Think about this:

In the early 1900s, if you saw a man walking down the street wearing a black hat and black suit, you might notice him, but he wouldn't look extremely out of place. And in the late 1900s, if you saw a man walking down the street wearing a black hat and black suit, you might notice him, but he wouldn't look extremely out of place. This particular outfit was flexible enough to work within the social context of a century or more. Therefore, if you are jumping around, traveling through time, and within the course of one "work day," you might find yourself visiting 1915, then 1989, then 1953, you could keep the same clothes all the while. This is a convenient suit that fits within the general fashion of an era—not specific enough to be quite right, but not so generally strange to draw undue attention. If the Paratemporal Loop Hypothesis is correct, then the MIB are future humans, slightly cyborg (with alien influence) who work to keep the secret of paratemporal contact and time travel for the benefit of future humans. In that regard, they are the most human of the paratemporals. Now of course, I don't mean to say there aren't regular old government spooks running around in black suits, as well. But there is much less of that than you might think.

Given that standard, non-paranormal government and military powers form the bulk of our system, and they thrive on creating confusion to maintain their secrecy, this whole thing is further complicated by low-level government taking advantage of the ridicule factor associated with people who discuss the paranormal. For example, let's say a military division is practicing how to secretly run through a civilian area at night, and they choose your backyard as a practice course before going into a live war zone. If your dog starts barking and you look outside to see men running by with rifles, you'll likely call the local police. But if those same men are wearing rubber alien masks, you might hesitate to pick up the phone and tell the local authorities that you've seen two aliens in your backyard. For this reason, I feel confident that governments often disguise their personnel and equipment in the guise of paranormal imagery from modern pop culture. It works.

The real paratemporals seem to have a fascination with human life forms, and especially blood. There were reports of Mothman chasing a bloodmobile and women on their periods. Chupacabra sucks blood. Cattle mutilations leave carcasses without blood. Again, it is not inconceivable that some of them are actually eating humans. The idea of the vampire itself is likely based on this fact. As Bram Stoker wrote, "The blood is the life." And when paratemporals appear, they often leave traces of radiation. First hand witnesses have shared records of radiation exposure and conjunctivitis with me. Massive radiation also has a tendency to settle in the anus, so mutilated cattle, with cored-out rectums, may demonstrate that someone is checking the carcasses to measure the amount. In many cases, cattle mutilation is just the product of natural decomposition with tiny insects and microorganisms eating the most sensitive parts of a highly symmetrical anatomy, creating the appearance of fine slices with a blade. But that, along with digestion of leaking fluids, does not explain something like radiation.

There are many ways in which strange beings manifest. And there are evidence and methods we can use to discern the real paratemporals from deceptions and illusions. But keep in mind that all of these phenomena may exist within those loops, so abundant that they enshroud our lives and the entire human experience. As you read these words, the world outside your window may essentially look the same, but just beyond your view, it is changing in some fundamental way.

Since we are talking about time travel, there is one other point that should be made. It is possible that those (or at least some of those) who travel into the past cannot interact with it. They might be invisible to us, or partially invisible, since their dimensional position may be close to ours but does not completely merge. If that is the case, they might appear as shadowy figures that quietly watch us—the infamous *shadow people*. As opposed to shadowy, phantasmal forms that might simply be ghosts that have not fully materialized, shadow people behave in a particular fashion that defines them. They tend to crouch back in a corner, or some other subtle nook, and watch us. Yet when they are noticed, they quickly exit. If from the future, this could explain why they run. They know that if you merely perceive them, it could influence the chain of events, altering the timeline, and jeopardizing the future.

There are other paratemporals that simply watch us, though. We enjoy stories about those we feel help us, angels and such. Yet some of the most frightening stories you can imagine come from those of a ghoulish nature. One story that raised the hair on my flesh was that of a young woman who moved into a haunted house. At first, she didn't know it was haunted. The first night, the she woke up at 2am sharp and sprang upright in bed. All seemed fine. The second, the exact same thing happened at 2am, and again the third night. After she told a co-worker, he suggested she set up a camera in the room, and he lent her his. That night, the same thing happened, but with the camera rolling this time. The next day, upon returning from work, she watched the footage. There she was, lying asleep in bed, all normal. Then, at 1:57am, a tall, black form, very similar to the grim reaper, quietly drifted up to her bedside. He stood there, silently watching her sleep until 1:59am. Then he turned and glided away. Moments later, she sprang upright at 2am.

Just as some of the paratemporals want our blood, others simply want our energy. If you see them, and are panicked, you withdraw your energy field. But when you don't see them, and are relaxed and at ease, your aura is wide and radiant. You're vulnerable, and it's easier for them to feed off your energy directly without your attention. The paratemporals that slip in and out of this realm sometimes orient themselves to humans, and take our orgone. So when one realizes that a paratemporal is trying to avoid observation, it is because that being is either a bio-feeder or is a partially-manifested time-traveler from the future attempting to stay hidden as he or she watches us for a variety of purposes.

This realm, this synchronistic fantasy, in which we perceive so much, yet are conscious of so little, is truly an overwhelming place. In the most technical sense, this very moment is all that really exists; the here and now, but how long is that moment? Time is indeed a flexible thing. Your time machine—the one between your ears—is processing data as quickly as it can. Your wormhole brain is sucking it in and shooting it out as rapidly as possible, the frequency changing all the while. And as the program runs through, where is it leading? What happens when you reach the end?

CHAPTER SEVEN
Your Purpose & Intention

HAVE YOU ever heard of a *tulpa*? It is a Tibetan term, and refers to a thought form, created by either a human, or humans, that is so powerful it eventually takes on its own independence. There are great examples of tulpas in recent history. Walter Gibson, who wrote *The Shadow* novels of the 1920s was prolific. From his house in Greenwich Village, he churned out an incredible number of books in a short period of time. For years afterward, residents claimed the place was haunted by his fictional characters. Another example is the "Philip Experiment." In the 1970s, a group of Canadian psychical enthusiasts decided to create a fictional ghost. They produced an elaborate back story about his origins, appearance, life, and death. Once he was vividly visualized, they referred to him from time to time as if he were real. After a few months, he indeed became real, and began to haunt them. Sometimes the outcome was even violent. Had some discarnate spirit stepped into the mold they created, or did they produce a tulpa? Believe it or not, every year adults around the world say they see Santa Clause. There is no logical reason to believe a man is flying around and dropping off presents, yet they actually, physically see him. It seems tulpas are real.

The idea of the tulpa is exciting on a number of levels. For one thing, it demonstrates the true power of the human mind. These anecdotes, if true, show us that one intense human mind, or a large mass of average minds, can influence the matter and energy around us in ways almost unimaginable. This is telekinesis of the highest degree. You can create your world in wondrous ways. And when I say *you*, I mean *you*, yes *you*!

The Heisenberg Uncertainty Principle has proven that you influence the world around you by simply observing it; so much so, that it actually causes a problem for scientific measurement. Your ability to create your reality, and shape the forces that flow around and through you, begins with thoughts. My friend Mobius is fond of retelling a profound experience he had years ago. As a fan of old sci-fi films, he always wanted to see a UFO. One night he went outside determined he would see one. He had put lots of thought and proper concentration into the exercise. As he watched the sky, his wish came true. There, blazing across the dark horizon, was a UFO. And, amazingly, it looked like an old, rickety rocket ship, containing rivets and all, with measly sparkles of flame spitting from the back as it meandered across the sky. He was stunned. Mobius knew that what he was seeing could not function aerodynamically, and yet he was watching precisely what he had grown up with. The UFO appeared as one of the crappy old models from a cheesy b-movie. He interpreted this affair as a practical joke being played on him by the universe, showing him, in an absurd and blatant form, that he possessed the power to shape his reality on levels that exceeded his wildest expectations.

The growing body of scientific knowledge that indicates we can create the reality around us has been called evidence of a "holographic universe." However, to be more precise, I prefer to call it a *holosentient* universe. What exactly does this mean? "Graphic" refers to that which can be visually appreciated, but "sentient" applies to a full presence, appreciable physically, visually, audibly, aromatically, and generally within all realms of perception. We are not talking about one's ability to just project some optical illusion. We are heralding the ability to manifest forms that are just as real, solid, palpable, vivid, and corporeal as any object in the room around you. This may seem unbelievable, but you must believe it. Here we go back to the concept of the magical Manifestor. If you want something, and you spend enough time seeing it clearly, you will eventually attract it or create it. That is why you must be careful about your daily attitude. Positive, selfless attitude and behavior create positive opportunities, and negative, selfish attitude and behavior create negative ones.

All of this may sound like the typical mumbo jumbo New Age talk you've heard for years, or read about in many other books by many other names. But let me present this from some angles you may not have considered. A computer is modeled on the human brain. It compartmentalizes and considers information in a similar fashion to how it seems to work in our heads. This is an example of how a human creation tends to mirror a human function. Let's expand this concept of a human brain to a cosmic brain; some sweeping mass of intelligence of which we are part. This seems much like the internet. The internet is real. Yet if I ask you, "Where is the internet?" what is your answer? As you should be able to immediately see, this is an invalid question because it shows a basic misunderstanding of the topics at hand. Asking "where is the internet?" is similar to asking someone "what color is the time?" The internet is not a particular place, but a flow of information. And that flow of information makes a tangible impact on our lives.

The universe is like the internet. It, too, is a flow of information. And because you are a part of that information, you can influence it, just as you can influence the internet by building your own website. You can't control the entire thing, but you can mold it somehow to reflect what is within you, and thereby draw the kind of attention you desire. We know the universe is conscious because *we* are conscious, and we are a part of the universe. This mass consciousness is what some call God. Remember that it's incorrect to see God as some particular omniscient, omnipotent, sentient being, modeled after a person, who sits on a cloud and passes judgment. What a boring job that would be. If you knew everything and had infinite power, then life would hold no impulse or excitement. Life is defined by motion, and motion entails change, creation and destruction. The idea of a paradise in which there is no struggle or challenge is a cold, still death—the cessation of motion. You could say, in the strictest technical sense, that life equals motion.

Though our society struggles with questions of abortion, execution and euthanasia, the most important facet is respect for the safety and comfort of fully-formed, healthy, conscious beings. In the practical limits of our worldly control, you are alive when you are independent and know you're alive, and you're dead when your awareness of life is gone for good. Though sad, some people must be executed from this plane, like serial killers and dictators. But altogether, all motion lives. There is no sense being a vegetarian, since plants live and feel just as animals. You must eat something living in order to live. Maybe someday we will not; we will exist in perfect energetic harmony with our surroundings once again.

Time and time again, believers in books like the Bible will give their opinion starting with, "But the Bible says . . ." Right off the bat, that person does not know what the Bible actually says. None of us do. The Bible was written in another language thousands of years ago by people who didn't know how a microwave worked, or that the earth was round. Over the centuries, it has been translated and re-translated, kept in secret by those few who were literate, and edited so it could be abused by rulers in the past who cited the Bible as their grant of power, abusing it then as so many still do today. Religion was the earliest form of government. In a time before people were deterred from committing crimes by DNA and computer tracking, the only way to preserve control was to tell them: maybe you think you're getting away with your sin, but there is a great invisible force always watching you, and he knows what you've done, and he'll make sure you pay for it one way or another! But there is no sense in arguing with the true believer. That person does not understand logic. Atheists are equally out of touch, as they have decided on something that cannot be known. They are so self-centered that they judge life's possibilities based on the tiny band of their human perception.

The only thing I can tell you for certain is that I popped out of a vagina some years ago, and I'm not 100 percent sure about that. Since then, everywhere I've turned, people have been telling me what is right and wrong, what I should and should not do. It's up to me to make a decision based on my guideline of who actually suffers if I do this or that incorrectly. But regardless of whether I began when I emerged from the womb, or I've been here all along, there exists some creative force that formed and propels me. And because I was created, I have a piece of that creation within. I am therefore a *creator*. And this is the meaning of life. The meaning of life is to give life meaning. What meaning will you give to yours? The holosentient universe allows you to make almost anything you like, using your thoughts to shape its flow of information.

Though we know that the invisible world is real, just as we know there are radio waves bringing voices into our radio speakers, it's still very difficult to completely embrace that which we cannot see. There are simple tools that are helping us see even these subtleties, though. Shutter speed is one reason photographs sometimes show us things that are otherwise invisible. If you turn on a fan at high speed, the blades may appear invisible. But if you photograph them at high speed, the picture shows them clearly. The same effect can be achieved using a strobe light, and this is why photography is often used at haunted places. Now we are playing with shutter glasses. These are plastic frames with LCD lenses that plug into a computer. When you look through them, you can punch whatever frequency you like into the computer, and the lenses will flash at that rate. At various frequencies, you can look around and see things in the world that you could not see with your direct vision alone. L.E.M.U.R. member Joe Southards provided our team with some shutter technology, and it was in a haunted cave in east Tennessee, during an investigation, that another one of my team members, Chris McCollum, discovered 100.11 hertz allowed some people to see dark, apparitional forms moving about the cave. The cavern was used as a hospital during the American Civil War. We now call these devices "ghost glasses."

And yet, what is proof? What is knowing? Is proof of ghosts a great photo of an apparition? We have tons of those. Is proof of ghosts a clear voice recorded in an empty room? We have plenty of those. There is much talk about proving paranormal phenomena, but what do you need to see? Maybe you simply need to experience something yourself to believe it. Fine—and when it happens, you can simply offer another one of the countless anecdotes to be dismissed by those who have not shared the experience. I am currently working on a computerized system that will record images at a place from four perspectives, along with electromagnetic and electrostatic data, only influenced by something that is physically present. But will this provide enough proof? Or shall we accept that no degree of proof can ever be attained? These things we call paranormal are, by their very nature, those things that will always elude the masses. Yet there is something paranormal about the very fact that we even exist, and this dreamscape around you right now is foreign to everything else found in the nature around us.

The reality of ghosts is based foremost on the human experience. Because we experience spirits, spirits are real. The human mind is the key. Whether you dream in black and white or color, your dream world is the real world while you sleep. And in that open state of mind, spirits from the past may visit you. Do they come from within you, slipping in through the Wormhole Brain? Probably. They most likely time travel into your seat of consciousness. Your world changes as your brain waves alter. You sleep in the very low delta state, relaxing you and opening you to new encounters. But just above that is the theta state, also very receptive, and one you can experience when you are not asleep, yet still open to psychic awareness and great mental feats. This is the state that monks enter when meditating, mathematicians engage when working on difficult problems, or athletes call upon when entering "the zone." You can automatically enter this state whenever you want using simple, domed eye coverings called Tibetan IMOs. See www.JoshuaPWarren.com for more information on how they work. But one of the best methods to encounter spirits with your mind is the psychomanteum.

The ancient Greek psychomanteum technique was rediscovered and modernized by Dr. Raymond Moody. It takes a mirror and a dimly lit room, and it works so well that many have life-changing experiences inside. The psychomanteum set up at our Lab in Asheville, North Carolina, is visited by people far and wide who desperately need to contact the other side. Though many people play white noise and make audio recordings, hoping a ghost will assemble those random particles into a voice—EVP—that method is far less satisfying than the interactions with full-bodied apparitions occurring in the psychomanteum, even though they are mental events. I am Certified in the Psychomanteum Method by the Raymond Moody Institute, and I have helped some people experience the paranormal in ways that transformed them forever. Mirror gazing and scrying create a closed circuit—you gaze into your own infinity. The realizations that come from this are profound.

Often an interviewer will ask me something like, "is there proof of the paranormal?" This is like saying "is there proof of dreams?" "The paranormal" is not a thing, it is a designation for phenomena that happen rarely and inconsistently, that break the requirements of scientific evidence, and are most deeply grasped by the human experience alone. In that regard, the paranormal will always be just beyond grasp, and the moment we can hold it, put it in a bottle or under a microscope, it no longer becomes paranormal, but normal. This is the curse of the paranormal investigator—one who devotes his or her life to those things that are always just beyond. If a Bigfoot were captured tomorrow, the primatologists would step in front of the cryptozoologists and say "we'll take it from here, thanks." And those who spent lives devoted to the thing when it was considered mere legend are left in the dark to chase their next phantom.

Sometimes, a thing is defined by its very lack of evidence. Modern physicists and cosmologists talk about dark matter and the dark flow. Dark matter is defined by the fact that it cannot be defined. It is some negative void, a vacuum of understanding, that is accepted because *something* is there, has to be there, *needs* to be there, to make all the other laws and theories work. But instead of revising the entire system, scientists are comfortable with acknowledging this behemoth that ties their loose ends together. It is the elephant in the room, and we are consumed with its effects while forced to acknowledge we cannot grasp the cause.

As I write this, my team and I are engaged in sensational research at our Lab. We have been able to produce a ray of energy ("The Ray") that seemingly does not respond to electricity, magnetism, radiation, or heat turbulence. Presently, we're not sure what it is. Using special Schlieren optical imaging, we're able to see it, but what are we seeing? Are we seeing something that we have created? Or are we seeing something that has always been there, will always be there, that appears to us only when everything around it is disturbed. It's like a rubbing on a tombstone, showing up because the charcoal marks everything around it, but not *it*. Maybe these rays are bands of material that connect all things in a very distinct way. They connect you to the coffee cup beside you, and connect our planet to the other heavenly bodies in space. Ultimately, this kind of study might clarify our relationship with the cosmos, illustrating that we are not connected to everything by wishes and philosophy alone, but by an actual web of networks, as plain and distinct as the resonant strings on a guitar. And those connections are so old and solid that they are not swayed by the flux of ambient energy, yet they snap from matter to matter, thought to thought, shifting around and throughout this holosentient universe. It could be that impressive ancient structures, like the pyramids, somehow utilized Ray Energy to facilitate the travel of paratemporals.

Allowing your mind to synchronize with the wonderful changes in the world, exciting your frequency to move into greater dimensions, will inspire you to create beneficial things. The greed of miserly energy barons has driven world poverty. Contrary to the strict capitalistic belief, hoarding all the wealth just because you can is not good, and eventually devalues wealth itself, generating terrible karma for the wealthy. Believe it or not, the surest way to guarantee wealth continues flowing your way is to be generous and continually give to *worthy* causes. But free energy is around us all, for us all, everywhere. Textbook perpetual motion machines may not be feasible, but virtual perpetual motion is. For example, a windmill turns so long as there is wind, and water wheels spin so long as there is water. Solar panels can be vastly improved, taking advantage of the amazing power blasting us each day. These resources should be developed and shared. Better yet, let us harness gyroscopic principles and pendulums to make devices that work independent of the earth's rotation, tapping into that rotation so they can whirl and generate energy from the potential difference in motion. Even kinetic energy from the chaos around us, the stray fields and vibrations, can be collected with screens, springs, and magnifiers to create usable motion.

Electrical theory taught in schools is truly flawed. Experimenting engineers find that charges in the lab behave differently than they do on paper. Space itself contains a realm of great potential energy that we have not fully tapped. This vacuum energy, from the ether, is here for us to utilize for our own good. And strange forces exist around charged objects, revealing aspects of how Quick Silvers fly. Study the neutron. It holds many secrets.

You can either believe that all ancient cultures, disconnected, were making up the same fairy tales, or that they were all truly experiencing the same kinds of amazing visitations. Science has now shown us that their sensational reports were technologically feasible, and so we face the serious prospect of the "mass return of visitors" they all foretold. As we move into, and through, the great convergence, you will see this thing called "The Quickening" continue to accelerate. It is the climaxing of a long chain of events, picking up speed as "novelty" condenses. Look up some of the Terrence McKenna videos online. Those who are aware have found tiny ways in which the cosmos speak, reminding them of our overall cohesion, meaning and ultimate purpose in the universe. For years, select people around the globe have become obsessed with "11:11," a time they frequently notice on the clock.

As it turns out, on December 21, 2012, the great convergence will begin at 11:11 UT (Universal Time). Properly reading and using numbers can open grand pathways into the secrets of time and space. We use numbers to count money, and there are magical practices, incorporating a particular number, that will help bring you wealth.

As you march forward in life, you should always remember that the big picture is the same as the little one. Grand bodies move around each other in space, just as tiny bodies move around each other within each cell and atom of your body. If a soccer ball were the size of earth, each atom would be the size of a pea. Imagine the massive, dynamic dimension your body holds. The universe and all its conflicts, concepts we call good and bad, waves of time travel, swirl inside you. You are as important as everything, and everything is there in you. This is because, through your Wormhole Brain, you are *connected* to it *all*.

We've really come full circle here. Thousands of years ago, shamans and mystics spoke of the spiritual component within humans, and our ability to communicate with the universe, by prayer or meditation. The scientific tradition began by dismissing the personalized human experience, and looking to the collective experiences, those things we could agree upon (like the weight of an object) called "objective." And now, as we proceed, we've found that the collective experience cherished by science has pointed us right back to the unique, human point of view. We just needed tools fine enough to measure the smallest motions, and minds large enough to see the full picture. By balancing the little picture with the big one, we now know they are one and the same. Every manmade object around you began as a thought in someone's head. You possess this power, too.

This holosentient universe is like a big computer program, or a matrix, swayed by forces past, present, and future, and minds great and small. As you move through this particular cycle, this thing you call your current life, you are like that ant on the Mobius Strip. Imagine yourself crawling across an enormous photograph. This photo represents what you have to learn and process in this life. You digest it day by day, like a tiny scanner, drawing it in pixel by pixel. And when you finally reach the end, when you hit the last pixel of the photo you've been sent, the entire thing—your whole life—flashes before your eyes. And then you understand. You have gathered the big picture, then you leave here, on to watch another slideshow in another place; the process starting again.

There is no beginning or end. You are here because you have to be somewhere, and where you go from here depends on what you gather from this vast photograph of life. It's a map that will show you where to go next. If you've done well and led a life full of friends, they may be waiting for you when you die, helping to guide you on to another adventure. But if you alienate others and treat them coldly, no one will help you progress, and you may find yourself lost and alone, frightened and confused. Keep your mind open to the complex beauty of this experience you have today, and judge it on your own, without cowering before others who have bought into, and clung onto, this temporary and fleeting world. All that you see around you is destined for decay, but your memories and spirit can live on, with positive direction. The meaning of life is to give life meaning. On each mirror of your house, post a reminder. Ask yourself, "What will I create today?" For you are, in fact, a paratemporal. Yes, you. This is the secret wisdom, secret no more.

For deeper understanding, read these books by Joshua P. Warren:

How to Hunt Ghosts

Pet Ghosts

And visit **www.JoshuaPWarren.com** and **ShadowboxENT.com** for movies, events & updates on new discovery.

BIBLIOGRAPHY

Abbot, Edwin A. *Flatland: A Romance of Many Dimensions*. England: Seely & Co., 1884.

Cosimano, Charles W. *Psychic Power*. St. Paul, MN: Llewellyn Publications, 1987.

--------. *Psionic Power*. St. Paul, MN: Llewellyn Publications, 1989.

Forstchen, William F. *One Second After*. New York: Forge, 2009.

Marrs, Jim. *Rule by Secrecy*. New York: Harper Collins, 2001.

Pye, Lloyd. *Everything You Know is Wrong*. Madeira Beach, Florida: Adamu Press., 1997.

Warren, Joshua P. *How to Hunt Ghosts*. New York: Simon & Schuster, Fireside, 2003.

----------. *Pet Ghosts*. Franklin Lakes, New Jersey: New Page Books, 2006.

INDEX

ABOUT THE AUTHOR

Joshua P. Warren is internationally recognized as an expert on mysterious and paranormal phenomena. He is the President of L.E.M.U.R. (League of Energy Materialization and Unexplained phenomena Research) based in the mountains of Asheville, North Carolina, founded in 1995. Warren has published ten books on the extraordinary, including the influential *How to Hunt Ghosts* (Simon and Schuster, 2003). He and his team made the cover of the science journal *Electric Space Craft* in 2004 for their work on understanding how plasmas similar to ball lightning are created in nature. He has spoken at international conferences on ghosts, cryptids, ESP, and UFOs. He's a regular guest on *Coast to Coast AM*, and hosts the Clear Channel radio program *Speaking of Strange*. Warren has produced and directed numerous films, including the controversial documentary *Inside the Church of Satan*, and has appeared on the History Channel, Discovery Channel, Travel Channel, TLC, Sci-Fi Channel, Animal Planet and National Geographic Channel. His work has also been covered by CNN, Fox News, *The New York Times*, and numerous news affiliates across the globe. Warren is often in the field, leading expeditions to enigmatic locations world-wide. Several popular tours, officially based on his work, are available in Asheville, drawing paranormal enthusiasts from around the country each year. See: www.JoshuaPWarren.com

LaVergne, TN USA
01 June 2010
184555LV00003B/6/P

9 780578 033945